FIGHTING INVISIBLE TIGERS

STRESS MANAGEMENT FOR TEENS

REVISED & UPDATED 4TH EDITION

EARL HIPP

free spirit
PUBLISHING®

Library of Congress Cataloging-in-Publication Data
Names: Hipp, Earl, 1944- author.
Title: Fighting invisible tigers : stress management for teens / Earl Hipp.
Description: Revised & updated fourth edition. | Minneapolis, MN : Free Spirit Publishing, [2019] |
    Includes bibliographical references and index. | Audience: Ages 11+
Identifiers: LCCN 2019008547 (print) | LCCN 2019980912 (ebook) | ISBN 9781631984358 (paperback) |
    ISBN 1631984357 (paperback) | ISBN 9781631984594 (epub) | ISBN 9781631984587 (pdf)
Subjects: LCSH: Youth—United States—Life skills guides—Juvenile literature. | Stress (Psychology)—
    Juvenile literature. | Stress (Physiology)—Juvenile literature
Classification: LCC HQ796 .H495 2019 (print) | LCC HQ796 (ebook) | DDC 305.2350973—dc23
LC record available at https://lccn.loc.gov/2019008547
LC ebook record available at https://lccn.loc.gov/2019980912

Edited by Brian Farrey-Latz
Cover and interior design by Shannon Pourciau
Illustrated by Dave Shephard

Free Spirit Publishing
An imprint of Teacher Created Materials
9850 51st Avenue North, Suite 100
Minneapolis, MN 55442
(612) 338-2068
help4kids@freespirit.com
freespirit.com

FSC
100%
From well-managed forests
www.fsc.org

Dedication

This book is dedicated to all young people who are fighting invisible tigers without help or support.

Acknowledgments

Writing is only one part of bringing a book into the world. It takes a publisher who "gets it," contributors, editors, artists, printers, and office and warehouse people, all doing their parts to bring this book into being and into your hands. I want to thank this whole crew for their special skills and contributions. You are all playing important roles in helping young people deal with the stress in their lives.

Some very special thanks to:

Judy Galbraith, the owner and president of Free Spirit Publishing, for her relentless commitment to the teachers and young people she serves with her high-quality product line. The hope that the educational system will someday change to allow for the full development of the human potential of all our kids is kept alive in people like her. I'm honored and proud to be connected to her and Free Spirit.

Brian Farrey-Latz and Marjorie Lisovskis, for their wizardly editorial skills, and **Shannon Pourciau**, whose fresh design brought excitement and energy to this new edition, along with the dynamic illustrations from **Dave Shephard**. It was a gift and pleasure working with them all.

All the young people who took the risk to share the hard and fun parts of their lives. Their honest quotes in this book will help other kids feel less alone with their invisible tigers.

My caring friends who together make up my Safety Net of Support. You make it easier to take the risk of putting myself out in the world.

All my family, including my wife, Gwen, for her unselfish support, and Clara and Naomi, two of my youth editors, for their teen and tween-age perspectives.

To a benevolent universe that somehow arranged all the coincidences required for me to be a writer at all and to have you reading this book. I'm blessed beyond my ability to understand, but I am eternally grateful.

CONTENTS

INTRODUCTION

Do you ever feel worried or stressed out? If so, you're not alone. Everyone feels upset or overwhelmed at times.

Facing one tough challenge at a time might be okay, but that's not how life usually works. Instead, one thing piles on top of another. In a single week you might have to finish a big project, take a few tests, perform in the school play, put in hours at your job, and do a bunch of other things. At the same time, you might also be dealing with situations that come up at home, troubles you have with friends, or any number of dramas that can come about from online social interactions.

Stress is the feeling you have when facing many challenges at the same time. Imagine every worry, tough homework assignment, health concern, relationship problem, awful online comment about you, and disagreement is a separate rubber band around your head. That would be very uncomfortable, right? But it can get worse. As more stressors show up, more rubber bands get layered on until your head is completely covered. The pressure you feel on the inside of that ball of rubber bands is stress.

Knowing where to start fixing things can be difficult because stress comes from all the pressures in your life. It's normal to feel anxious and uncomfortable every day when you're feeling stressed—like something is wrong—even though you can't say exactly what it is.

STRESS OVERLOAD

Dealing with a lot of stress can make people feel cornered—like there's nowhere safe to turn. Making good decisions under this kind of pressure can be difficult. Instead of calmly coming up with solutions to a problem, feelings of tension or anger can get in the way and cause people to do things that make a situation worse.

Fighting Invisible Tigers

When you're stressed out, it can feel like you're in a thick jungle with lots of dangerous tigers—ferocious, hungry, but invisible tigers. You can't see them, but you can sense them quietly stalking you.

Imagine . . .

You're alone in a steamy jungle. You've been hacking through it for days while huge mosquitoes chomp at your flesh. Weird noises and strange smells fill the air. Every now and then you hear a deep, menacing growl . . . and you worry what's going to happen next.

Now imagine living with this fear every day—always watchful, always on edge and ready to react in an instant. That's how a person who doesn't know how to handle stress can feel. Being on guard every minute takes an enormous amount of energy—whether it's watching for real tigers or invisible ones in the form of tests, homework, bullying, friendship fallouts, or other stressors. Constant worrying about what might happen next is exhausting and can push you to your physical and emotional limits.

STRESS IS SERIOUS BUSINESS
High levels of stress over long periods of time can have severe effects. You might begin to feel aches and pains and get sick more often. Your performance at school and in other activities may suffer. Your relationships can fall apart. Stress can also affect your moods, you might start to feel angry, sad, lonely, or depressed.

The bad news is you can't keep stressors out of your life completely—situations will come up that cause you to feel uncomfortable, frustrated, or overwhelmed. The good news is you can learn more about stress and positive ways to deal with the challenges and hard times. You can learn how to fight the invisible tigers when they do show up.

How Can This Book Help?

The goal is to help you stay healthy, meet challenges, feel great about yourself, and make the most of your life. *Fighting Invisible Tigers* offers ideas you can use to really understand stress and handle it in positive ways:

"Stress 101: The Lowdown on Invisible Tigers" has information on stress and its physical and emotional effects. You'll read about some of the unhealthy ways people deal with feeling overwhelmed and learn the important difference between short-term coping techniques and real stress management.

In **"11 Tiger-Taming Techniques"** you'll learn about important skills you can use to manage stress—helpful strategies you can start using right now to relieve some of the pressure you feel and to prepare for future challenges. The "Manage Digital Tigers" section offers strategies for managing stressors in the digital world—problems that can come from spending lots of time online.

And finally, **"First Aid for Tiger Bites"** has helpful suggestions for when you feel like you've hit your limit. If you're feeling upset or overwhelmed right now, you can check out this section (page 127).

Reading this book will not make you an expert tiger tamer overnight, but practicing the many stress management skills it describes can help you make your invisible tigers seem smaller and much less ferocious. I sincerely hope that with the skills to manage some of the stress in your life, your heart, mind, and spirit will be more open to the opportunities and joys waiting for you.

Good luck and my very best wishes go with you on your adventure.

Earl Hipp

P.S. I like hearing from my readers. If you're willing to share, I'd enjoy hearing about how you're doing and what you're learning. I may even be able to help others by sharing your thoughts in my books and presentations. Feel free to send your comments or questions to me in care of:

Teacher Created Materials
PO Box 1040
Huntington Beach, CA 92647

Or email me at help4kids@freespirit.com.

THE LOWDOWN ON INVISIBLE TIGERS

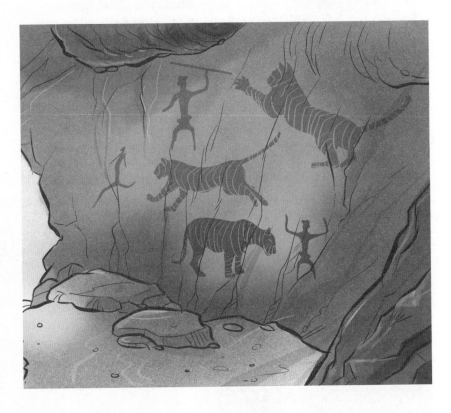

Stress may seem like a modern phenomenon, but actually it's been around for millions of years. Even in the times of cave-dwelling humans, people struggled with problems that made life complicated, difficult, and frightening—fires that wouldn't start, bad weather, spoiled meat, damp caves, unruly neighbors, grumpy family, and the challenges of simply surviving. But the most serious stressors for cave dwellers were the wild animals that saw them as, well, lunch.

5

The Fight, Flight, or Freeze Response

On a nice day in the jungle, for example, a huge hungry saber-tooth tiger could suddenly leap at the cave dwellers.

> **THE POWER OF FIGHT, FLIGHT, OR FREEZE**
> The fight, flight, or freeze response is so sensitive that simply thinking about hungry tigers or any other frightening things can get your body fired up and ready to instantly react.

Because most tigers are in no mood for conversation, these early humans learned to react instantly to either attack the cat or run for safety. This required a finely tuned nervous system that could mobilize the body into what we now call the fight, flight, or freeze response. Over millions of years, the people with the best fight, flight, or freeze skills lived on to tell stories around the fire, and the others . . . let's just say they didn't make it home for dinner.

While most of us will never have to face real tigers, the world we live in can feel every bit as threatening as the one that cave dwellers experienced. Think about it for a moment: There are a lot of situations that can make us feel upset or seriously threatened.

> The environment is being destroyed—will we even have a place to live in 50 years?

> Since we moved to this town, I haven't been able to make friends.

> I lost my phone—it had all my contacts in it.

My life is drama central. Justine hates me and Maria says I stepped in on her crush.

Someone was stabbed in my neighborhood and I'm afraid to walk alone.

I'm overweight and everybody in my class ignores me.

There's a guy at school who thinks I'm his personal punching bag.

When I see Sam using and selling, I get scared he'll go to jail like his brother.

I have no idea what I'm going to do with my life when I finish school.

I have a huge test next week that makes up half my biology grade.

I get sad when I see starving people on TV.

My parents had a major fight—Mom moved out.

Some challenges definitely are more difficult to deal with than others. But the problem is, whenever you're up against something, anything that makes you feel worried or threatened—even if you're just thinking about it—your body still responds as if it's meeting a hungry tiger. At the first hint of trouble, the alarm goes off, and instantly your body gets ready to fight, run away, or lock up in paralysis.

During times of high stress, the fight, flight, or freeze response causes many physical changes in your body—all at the same time—and if you don't understand what's happening, it might feel like you're having a serious medical problem.

Effects of Fight, Flight, or Freeze

Here are some of the ways your body might react to a major stress event in your life:

Your heart pounds. The body needs all the oxygen-rich blood it can get, and it needs it in a hurry, so your heart pumps harder and faster. Your breathing also speeds up to make more oxygen available.

Your hands and feet become cold. Small capillaries in the hands and feet constrict to force blood toward the brain to keep you alert and also into the large muscles used for running and fighting.

There is a rush of warmth to your face. The carotid arteries in the neck open up to allow more blood to the brain, sometimes causing the cheeks and ears to turn pink. You might get a pressure headache, or your face will feel hot.

Your mouth gets dry and your stomach feels upset. During fight, flight, or freeze, the digestion process shuts down, so blood is available for the body's largest running and fighting muscles. You may feel tingly or have "butterflies" in your stomach.

You feel restless. Glands and organs produce chemicals—including adrenaline—that help you become more aware, focused, and prepared to move fast. You'll feel restless, be impatient, and might find your feet tapping away.

Your hands sweat. Anticipating the extra heat that running and fighting generate, the body turns on its climate-control system and produces moisture on the surface of the skin. Evaporation of this moisture creates a cooling effect.

You go blank. When escape by flight (getting away from the problem) or fighting to survive aren't possible, you may become immobilized—physically, mentally, or even emotionally. This reaction is called disassociation and it can happen to anyone. When we can't deal with the challenge we're facing, our brains "shut down" and disconnect from the situation. It's like we're playing dead and hoping the danger will just pass.

It's important to remember that all of these reactions are normal responses for *anyone* encountering a big tiger, a major stress event, or more stressors than they're able to handle. No one is immune to these physical and emotional reactions when they are facing something they perceive as a serious danger.

STRESS AFFECTS YOUR MIND

Stress not only causes changes to your body, but it can also cause your brain to short-circuit. When you feel totally stressed, the decision-making part of your brain can go offline as stress chemicals flood your system. So, what does this mean? When you're stressed, you are a lot more likely to feel confused, make bad decisions, do things in a panic, or freeze up with inaction. These are all reactions that can make a situation worse. Teens are especially affected by this process because their brains are developing very quickly and changing during adolescence.

STRESS AFFECTS YOUR EMOTIONS

When your body is flooded with stress chemicals causing all kinds of bodily sensations and your brain is going a hundred miles an hour trying to figure out what to do next, your emotions can light up and add to your anxiousness. If you're operating at your limits, feelings of fear, hopelessness, sadness, restlessness, confusion, or a sense of being lost can be common.

Short- and Long-Term Stress

The fight, flight, or freeze response can take a lot out of you because fighting tigers—real or imaginary—is a whole body-mind-emotion experience. Fortunately, most periods of intense stress don't usually last very long. After the immediate danger of a stressful event passes, the body gradually calms down and enters a period of rest and recuperation before returning to a normal state. This is called short-term stress.

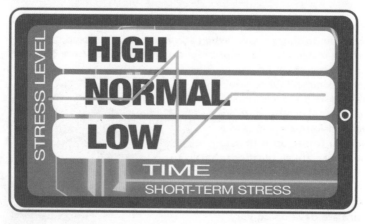

Short-term stress usually passes pretty quickly and without a lasting impact. But what happens if you have a lot of things causing stress in your everyday life? What if your life is full of invisible tigers—large and small—that don't ever seem to go away?

When you're experiencing lots of stressors over long periods of time, your body doesn't have time to calm down, rest, and recuperate after every stressful thing that happens. This is called long-term stress. Because you want to keep going, it's easy to adapt to higher and higher stress levels without realizing it. You might think you are doing okay, but you're actually living with an unhealthy amount of stress. This is why long-term stress can be so harmful—people don't realize the toll it's taking physically, mentally, and emotionally. Then, one day, they suddenly reach their limit and something lets go.

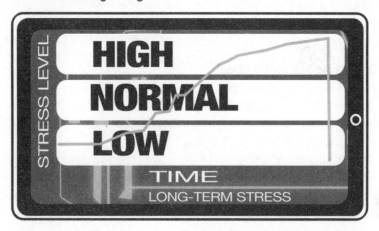

Seriously stressed people are usually trying to stay on top of things—even when they feel stalked by invisible tigers. But at some point, constant high levels of stress will become overwhelming. You will be trying harder and harder to keep up with all the challenges you're facing while—without realizing it—you're gradually losing physical energy, the ability

STRESS AND PIMPLES
While many effects of stress are quite serious, others can simply be annoying. For example, some researchers believe there is a link between stress and pimples. In the largest-ever study on acne and stress, teens with high-stress lives were 23 percent more likely to have their acne get worse. Apparently, when you're stressed, your skin knows it, and may react with angry eruptions.

to think clearly, and your performance edge. It's like chopping wood with an ax and never taking time to sharpen the blade or trying to stream a video using an internet connection that is getting slower and slower. Eventually, things that were easy become more difficult.

GET HELP!

If you feel like you're reaching your limit, it's important to talk with someone you trust—like a parent, teacher, or friend—right away. The person you share with might have solutions to challenges you haven't thought of. See "First Aid for Tiger Bites" (pages 127–130) for more ideas about what to do when you're feeling overwhelmed.

Coping Strategies

Life is full of situations to deal with—responsibilities at home, schoolwork, figuring out where you fit in, friendships. And then there are the unexpected stressors that can happen at any time. So how do you cope? What is "coping" anyway?

Think of coping as the short-term approach to dealing with the feeling of being stressed. Coping behaviors don't fix the problems that cause stress, but they can give you temporary relief from anxious feelings. There's nothing wrong with most coping activities— things like watching TV or napping—as long as they aren't harmful and don't go on forever.

What are some of these short-term actions people use to cope with feelings of stress? There are three basic categories: Distraction, Avoidance, and Escape.

1. Distraction—Or, I'll deal with it later.

"When I need a breather, I go for a bike ride."
—Sarah, 12

"At the end of a long day, I like to go online to see what people are up to. It helps me decompress from all the stuff that's happened to me."—Mario, 14

Distractions are the most common coping activities. They're usually pretty harmless and include things like hanging out online, reading, eating, or playing video games—pretty much any activity that allows you some time away from stressors. Distractions can be good for short-term relaxation and can even be productive. For example, taking a short break for a snack while studying is a way to briefly get away and come back with clearer focus. But taking too many breaks—such as to text your friends or chat online— won't get your work done and can increase the stress you feel.

Distractions help you avoid feeling stressed for a little while, but the more you use them to procrastinate, the more the stress you're avoiding creeps to the surface. That's often when people move on to the next level of coping.

2. Avoidance—Or, I might deal with it . . . sometime.

"My friends and I are pretty intense basketball players. We could play hoops all night."—Kwame, 13

"I admit it—when I don't want to do something, I go online. It's weird because I seem to get lost in time. Sometimes I look at the clock and it's hours later." —Brie, 14

Think of avoidance as distractions carried to the extreme—like when watching a little TV becomes watching every night for hours and hours. It's when a simple activity starts to take up more and more of your time and energy and causes you to put off dealing with things you're worried about or don't want to do. Unfortunately, this can lead to a *vicious circle* of behavior. That's when distractions pretty much take over your life. For example, hanging out with friends is great and can be an effective way to de-stress. But spending all your time with friends—day and night, in person or online—to distract yourself from difficulties at home or school can become a stress-generating and self-destructive pattern of avoidance.

Overachievement. Some serious avoidance activities can appear to be positive. For example, people who are bothered by some deep problem may get super-involved in activities and over-achieve to try to overcome negative feelings they have. They may excel in the classroom, be star athletes, and stay active in many school clubs. People who do this may seem to be totally together, but all of their activity is just a way to avoid dealing with the main problem.

People who overachieve often don't have the time, energy, or awareness to address the root feelings of stress. This can quickly become a vicious circle—the more time spent staying busy, the worse a person might feel. The worse they feel, the more active they become. Around and around it goes in a spiral, down into a deeper and deeper hole of exhaustion and isolation. Vicious circles can close in from all sides, growing tighter and tighter. Because the people affected are so concentrated on trying to keep it all together, they may not notice things steadily getting worse.

Procrastination. Pretty much everyone puts off boring or hard tasks from time to time. Some of the smartest, most motivated, and successful people are known (or secret) procrastinators. When you occasionally put off things, you can pretty much survive—even if it means a late night of studying at some point. But continuously using procrastination as an avoidance strategy can invite a vicious circle—one where mountains of things pile up for you to do, and you develop more drastic ways to avoid facing it all. Before long, you might have a stress-filled mess of missed deadlines, poor excuses, and confused priorities.

Procrastination is most dangerous when it becomes a way of avoiding the hardest parts of life—like tough problems at home, breakdowns in your relationships, or difficulties at school. When you put off dealing with hard problems or emotions, you can find yourself living with high levels of anxiety or confusion. You might end up feeling panicked or isolated until something inside you breaks. It's like slowly shaking a can of soda. Things look the same from the outside, but when you pop the tab—POW—you have one big, nasty mess on your hands.

Illness. Another avoidance strategy is using sickness to avoid the hard parts of life. Many students learn as little kids that illness is an acceptable reason to miss school—wasn't it nice to sleep in and chill out in front of the TV because you were "sick"? While it's tempting to take advantage of this strategy today, it's a risky play to use illness to avoid difficult situations.

STRESS AND SICKNESS
Faking illness can turn into a vicious circle of real, stress-driven health problems. Headaches, digestive problems, allergies, muscle pain, high blood pressure, eating disorders, chronic fatigue, and depression are only some of the many serious stress-related conditions.

For example, one of the main reasons students avoid school is out of fear—fear that they will be hurt, teased, or harassed by others. Bullying is a serious problem in many schools, but it is not an excuse to drop out. It can be hard to speak up about the person sending nasty texts about you or the kid who shoves your head into lockers, even if that's the best approach. What is the alternative? To avoid dealing with it by faking aches and pains to stay home? Each time you skip you fall further behind in your classes. Meanwhile, the main source of your stress—the situation at school—goes unresolved and adds to the tension you feel.

Sleep. It's normal to want to sleep in on Monday morning or to take an occasional nap. Most teens don't sleep the nine to ten hours each night their bodies need, so getting some solid sack time is actually a good thing. It can be a problem, however, if you stay in bed to hide out from stress-causing situations rather than reach out for help.

Sleeping for 12 hours night after night or not leaving your bed on weekends isn't healthy, because your problems can become more serious the more you sleep. Sleeping doesn't fix the problems you're facing, so they are still there when you wake up. As the challenges you face become more serious, you may want to sleep more until the effects of stress actually make it difficult to get out of bed.

Isolation. As your world gets more stressful and you feel tiger breath on the back of your neck, it's natural to want to retreat to a place where you feel safe. Withdrawing from the world for a while to regroup can be very good for you. But when you close your door and never come out, healing and restful withdrawal can become dangerous isolation. Even if you don't have a room of your own, you can shut out other people by ignoring them, not being around, or refusing to engage in any way. If a little time out becomes a need to always be alone, you may be caught in a vicious circle of isolation.

When you use isolation as a way to avoid invisible tigers, you lose the support and objectivity everyone needs when they're dealing with hard situations. When you're alone with your thoughts, negative or destructive thinking can sabotage your self-esteem and leave you feeling hopeless or depressed.

3. Escape—Or, I don't want to deal with it . . . ever.

"I made a bad mistake a couple years ago when things were intense. I'm in juvenile detention now and I miss being home."—Bobby, 15

"Sometimes I wish I could drop out—of school, of life, everything."—Cham, 14

Escapist behaviors can occur when you reach the limit of your ability to cope with the world around you, when you're at the edge of what you can handle. You've done the best you can to deal with the challenges you're facing, using the tools you have, but it's not enough. You're scared, overwhelmed, maybe embarrassed that you can't handle things, and you feel like all you can do is

SEVERE ESCAPIST BEHAVIORS
- skipping or dropping out of school
- running away from home
- using alcohol or other drugs
- addiction to food, sex, gambling, or the internet
- over-involvement in academics, sports, and other activities
- hurting other people
- lying to people as a way of life
- injuring yourself or attempting suicide

check out. Engaging in any escape behaviors is a sign you have lost your way, and you should get help immediately.

When you're feeling overwhelmed, hopeless, and at your limit, escape can feel like the only option. But escapist behaviors always make a bigger mess of your life and don't solve the underlying issues. They also generate mountains of additional problems that can burden you for years . . . maybe the rest of your life.

Relying on coping activities is like using your finger to plug a leak in a dam. It works for a while, but then the growing pressure behind the dam breaks through in another place, and another, and another. At some point, you run out of fingers. While these coping activities can be helpful in the short term, they are not a replacement for stress-management techniques you'll read about in the next section. For now, let's take a look at some myths about stress—and the final word on the subject.

GET HELP!

If you're involved in or moving toward any escapist behaviors, find someone you trust who you can talk to about what's going on. Remember: Asking for help when you're up against more than you can handle is not a sign of weakness. It's a sign of personal strength and having the courage to make things better. You might start the conversation by saying, "I'm having trouble with some parts of my life. Can I talk with you about how I'm feeling?" See "First Aid for Tiger Bites" (pages 127–130) for more ideas for getting help.

10 Myths and the Truth About Stress

Some myths about stress actually make it more difficult for you to successfully manage the challenges you're facing. Believing any of the following myths is a sure way to let invisible tigers gain on you.

10 Myths About Stress

Myth #1. I must be crazy for thinking and feeling the way I do. You're not crazy. Stress can cause anyone to have frightening thoughts and uncomfortable feelings. It's not that anything is wrong with you, just that your life is full of challenges and you're still learning the best ways to manage the stresses in your life.

Myth #2. I need to handle these fears and problems by myself—if I ask for help it proves I'm not smart or good enough. Actually, the opposite is true. Trying to handle tough situations alone most often leads to bigger problems. Reaching out for help when you need it is always the smartest way to stay healthy and perform at your best.

Myth #3. No one will understand how I feel. It's true that some of the important people in your life may not exactly understand your worries or know how to help, but someone will. If one person doesn't take you seriously, reach out to others until you find someone who does.

Myth #4. I can think my way out of feeling bad. Unfortunately, this isn't true. Feelings are nonintellectual, which means no amount of thinking can help you change them. When we're thinking about stressful situations, what we're usually doing is worrying. Worrying doesn't solve problems and only makes you feel worse. Like playing the same song over and over, worrying is just repeating thoughts about bad things that might happen. Endlessly rehearsing your fears will quickly wear you down.

Myth #5. If I keep busy, I'll feel better about myself. Staying active can help you avoid dwelling on some small worries. But the big problems—those responsible for the major stress in your life— won't go away until you face and deal with them in a constructive way. In fact, staying super active can lead to vicious circles (see page 13) and gradually make you feel worse over time.

Myth #6. If I can get through today, tomorrow is bound to be better. Maybe, and maybe not. It's possible that letting some time pass will make your concerns seem smaller or less serious. But it's also true that avoiding problems as a long-term solution can lead to situations getting worse. Living with stress every day also leaves you with less energy and sharpness to deal with the day's challenges. The best strategy is to deal with negative feelings as soon as you're aware of them.

Myth #7. I should be able to figure out things by myself. Who says? Being in the middle of a stressful situation is the hardest time to know what to do to make things better. Trying to figure it out alone cuts you off from the knowledge, experience, and support of others. That's why getting the outside perspective of a counselor, family member, friend, or trusted adult can put you on the path toward feeling better.

Myth #8. Life is so serious. Life does have many serious moments, but not balancing the pressure of these times with fun, rest, and relaxation will only make the hard times that much harder. You deserve to feel good about yourself and the life you have.

Myth #9. All I need is to be left alone for a while. Being alone can be helpful sometimes. But if your way of dealing with major stress in your life is to be by yourself and avoid talking to anyone, you can quickly get out of touch with reality and your support system.

Myth #10. I don't have time to try or practice stress-management techniques. The basics of stress management relate to activities you're probably already doing every day—things like eating well, getting exercise and rest, and having fun. Learning about a few tiger-taming skills—like time management, relaxation, mindfulness exercises, and goal setting—can help you have even more quality time.

And Now, the Absolute, Bottom-Line Truth About Stress . . .

There is no stress in the world.

That's right: There is no stress in the world. Surprised? Think about it. Where would you go looking for it if you wanted to find stress? Los Angeles? The Gobi Desert? Google? The bottom of your book bag? Chengdu, China? Stress just isn't anywhere "out there."

Stress is something that happens inside people—inside you. It's the result of how you think and feel about your experiences and challenges you face. To understand this better, imagine yourself in these two situations:

1. You're at the zoo having a great time when a person on the staff asks you to help feed the tigers—even though you have no training with animals. You look at the tigers, the tigers look at you (lunch!). Somehow you're not all that excited to help feed the tigers.

2. You're at the zoo minding your own business when you're asked to help feed the tigers. Luckily, you've graduated from Zoo Keeper School with high honors. You have all the skills and expertise you need to do the job, and you confidently enter the tiger sanctuary.

In each scenario, the tigers are the same. What's different is how you perceive them. And that depends on the skills you bring to the situation. For example, a test you haven't studied for probably makes you anxious. But the same test, after solid preparation, can seem like a piece of cake. It's the same with a lot of life's stressful moments. Having the right skills can make the difference between stress overload and really enjoying your life. The next section explains some of these very important tiger-taming skills.

FIND OUT MORE

TeensHealth (teenshealth.org). This website has a lot of advice on dealing with stress as well as many other health concerns. Visit the site to find articles, teen stories, and resources.

11
TIGER-TAMING TECHNIQUES

Listening to music, hanging out at the mall, shooting hoops, and other coping activities can take your mind off worries for a short time, but any stressful challenges you face are still there when the song ends or you go home. Stress-management skills, on the other hand, can help you become more grounded, confident, and stress-resilient and give you tools to handle future pressures. What are stress-management skills? This section features a collection of proven Tiger-Taming Techniques.

#1 GET MOVING
Ideas for keeping active to stay on top of stress—page 25.

#2 FIGHT STRESS WITH FOOD
Nutrition information you can use to feel your best—page 31

#3 FIND YOUR CALM CENTER
Relaxation skills that are good for your body and mind—page 39.

#4 STAND UP FOR YOURSELF

Assertiveness skills that can help reduce the stress you feel—page 55

#5 WEAVE A SAFETY NET OF SUPPORT

Suggestions for building strong relationships with friends and family—page 65.

#6 TAKE CHARGE OF YOUR LIFE

How to set goals and work toward making your dreams come true—page 75.

#7 GET TIME ON YOUR SIDE

Using time-management tips to sidestep stress—page 85.

#8 RISK TRYING NEW THINGS

Positive ways to challenge yourself and keep moving forward—page 93.

#9 STAND ON SOLID GROUND

Learning how to make decisions that are right for you—page 101.

#10 CHOOSE THE UPSIDE VIEW

Learning to see what's positive about yourself and the world around you—page 109.

#11 MANAGE DIGITAL TIGERS

How to make the most of technology while keeping screens from eating you alive—page 117.

Maybe you already use some of these techniques, others might not be familiar to you. This section gives you the opportunity to try all the techniques and find those that work best for you.

JAMIL, 13

Sometimes when my brothers are fighting and yelling, I take myself out for a long walk to calm myself down . . . even if it's raining. I always feel better afterward.

After my workout, I feel like I have more energy for the rest of the day. If I miss my routine, I start to feel sluggish and I have trouble getting things done.

KARNA, 14

REBECCA, 16

Sports are my outlet—I couldn't live without them.

I go to the boxing gym in my neighborhood. Twenty minutes on the heavy bag is a perfect outlet when I'm super angry.

OKUGN, 16

KEVIN, 15

I go for a swim when I start to feel tense. Every time I hit the pool, I lose a lot of the negative junk in my head and my mind becomes more clear.

#1
GET MOVING

Regular physical activity is one of the best stress-management skills. It's especially helpful during high-pressure times when your body is filled with fight, flight, or freeze chemicals and raring to go. By doing almost any physical activity, you use up some of the cortisol and other stress chemicals your body produces. If you're not active at these times, you can feel nervous, restless, uncomfortable, and even ill.

Some Benefits of Physical Activity

The positive health effects of regular physical activity do not end at relieving your body of stress-producing chemicals. Exercise also produces other chemicals—including endorphins—that help you feel good. Just putting your body in motion can help you feel more mellow and improve your mood. That's why after an especially hard day, a little physical activity can help you slow down, relax, and even sleep better.

Physical activity also has a huge impact on your health. In fact, being regularly active can change your entire body chemistry. As your fitness level improves, your body gets better at turning calories into energy—which means you store less fat on your body and use more of the energy stored in the foods you eat. The overall impact: You're not as hungry, you eat less, and you naturally crave foods that are better for you.

Your heart, lungs, muscles, and other vital parts of your body also become stronger and more efficient when you're active— researchers have shown that regular physical activity can add years to your life. Over time, feeling good about how you treat your body can also lead to higher self-esteem and feeling like you're taking charge of your life.

The FIT Formula for Physical Activity

How can you tell whether you're active enough? One way to get on the right track is to create a personalized activity program. You can do this using the FIT Formula. This formula helps you build a physical activity program that's right for you.

FIT FORMULA

F stands for Frequency—the number of times per week you do your activity.

I stands for the Intensity level you choose for the activity.

T stands for Time—how long your activity sessions last.

Frequency

In the United States, the federal government recommends at least one hour of physical activity most days of the week, preferably daily. The good news is that this activity doesn't have to be a chore. Qualifying activities can be just about anything that gets you moving. In fact, one health campaign focused on teens playing with a yellow bouncy ball—not too intense. If playing with a yellow ball isn't your thing, then walk, swim, dance, skateboard, bike, shoot hoops, throw a Frisbee, or do any other activity that's easy to make a habit.

Intensity

You may be tempted to go faster or farther or compete with others—or compete with yourself—by constantly pushing to exceed previous results. Wanting to perform well is okay but pushing yourself too hard can lead to fatigue or injury. And having fitness expectations that are too high can become another source of stress in your life. If you always overdo the intensity of your activity, it can become an uncomfortable chore.

The best way to avoid burning out or injuring yourself is to find a level of intensity that is just right for you. One easy-to-remember rule of thumb: If you can carry on a conversation during your workout, you're probably at a good intensity level. Inviting a friend to join you for a workout is a great way to monitor your intensity—and to keep you motivated.

A more scientific way to gauge the intensity of your activity session is to monitor your target heart rate (THR) while you are active. Your ideal THR is the specific pulse rate at which you receive the maximum benefit from your activity to build fitness and reduce stress. Contrary to popular belief, working harder is not necessarily better. You can figure out your target heart rate using this formula:

THR FORMULA

(220 − your age) X 0.7 ÷ 6
= Your THR for a 10 second count

The first part of the formula—(220 – your age) x 0.7—determines your target heart rate per minute. You divide it by six because when you check your pulse, you only count for 10 seconds. After that, a healthy heart is already beginning to return to its normal, inactive rate.

To find out if you're close to your THR, spend about 20 minutes at your chosen physical activity. Then check your pulse rate using your wrist or the carotid artery along the side of your neck. Look at a watch and count the beats for 10 seconds to see if you're in the zone . . . or at least within a few beats of your ideal number.

- If you're above your target heart rate or out of breath, you're probably pushing yourself too hard. Try slowing down the next time you work out.

- If you're below your target heart rate, you might be taking it too easy. To get full benefit from your activity, try increasing your pace before checking your THR again.

- If you are at or close to your target heart rate, you've found the intensity level you want to maintain during your activity sessions.

Being in motion at a pace that's comfortable for you will help you stick with an activity and avoid injury. At the right intensity level, your activity should be an enjoyable, relaxing, and stress-free part of your day that you look forward to.

MOTIVATION
Looking for a little motivation to get up and get moving? Try an exercise app. There are many free apps that help you log activities, track progress, and teach you new ways to stay in shape (like yoga). Many of these apps will also nudge you when it's time to start moving.

Time

To get the most out of any physical activity session, you need to keep your heart going at or near your target rate for a minimum of 20 to 30 consecutive minutes. A "work-hard-then-take-it-easy" approach won't give you the maximum benefit of activity. And don't forget to spend a few minutes stretching and warming up before an activity and cooling down afterward to keep your flexibility and avoid injury.

If you're not sure how to start your activity program, you might get some inspiration and guidance from a health or physical education teacher. It's also a good idea to check in with your doctor.

FIND OUT MORE

Presidential Youth Fitness Program (pyfp.org). A program managed by the National Fitness Foundation, the Presidential Youth Fitness Program encourages teens to participate at any activity level to improve their fitness. Visit the website for fitness calculators, activity logs, and other tools to help you establish your physical activity program and to track your progress.

Topics to search online:
- What are endorphins and endocannabinoids?
- What's my target heart rate while working out?
- What are the best fitness apps for teens?

MARCOS, 13

I've been overweight since fourth grade. Only with the help of a nutrition program have I started to feel healthier.

I used to think that I didn't have time for real meals and healthy snacks. Now that I'm used to feeling better from eating real food, I don't think I could ever go back.

JILLIAN, 15

OMAR, 14

I know it's not good for me, but I need a caffeine and sugar rush in the morning to get my day started.

It's harder to find good food, but the extra effort is worth it. Decent meals keep my body healthy and let me focus at a higher level.

RIYANNA, 16

FIGHT STRESS
WITH FOOD

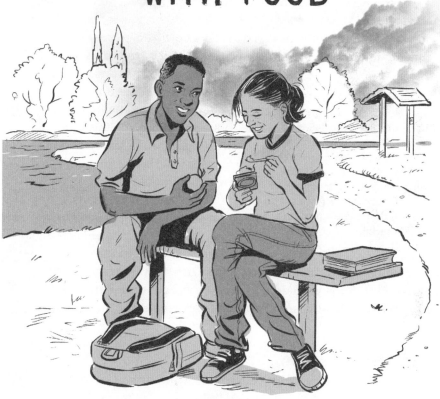

If you want to be a high-energy, active person who can manage stress, you'll need to put the right fuel in your tank. Eating a lot of different healthy foods—like fruits, vegetables, and whole grains—gives you the vitamins, minerals, protein, and other nutrients your body needs to function at its highest levels. Many other food options, sometimes those easiest to find, aren't good for your health. A poor diet can lead to conditions like diabetes and obesity and actually increase feelings of stress.

Why Is Eating Healthy So Important?

All the cells in the body are affected by the foods you eat. Every bodily action, from the way an injury heals to how well you're able to focus, is dependent on the performance of these cells.

For example, the 100 billion cells in your brain rely on proteins and vitamins to communicate and work together. The levels of these and other nutrients in your diet can affect how well you're able to concentrate during a stress-packed test. Healthy foods also give you the energy you need to perform at a high level. The bottom line: Your cells can tell the difference between what's healthy and what's junk, and you're not going to be at your best if you don't treat them right.

FRESH FRUITS AND VEGGIES
Fresh produce is better for you than processed foods made in a factory. Most ready-made fruit and vegetable food products, such as fruit juices and chips, contain only small amounts of natural materials. They are also often high in fat, sugars, and artificial additives.

The typical teen needs between 2,200–2,800 daily calories, including increased amounts of calcium, protein, iron, and other important nutrients to be healthy. Growth spurts can affect the number of calories you need, so it's important to discuss diet with a school nurse or healthcare provider at regular checkups.

Bad Diet Habits

While vegetables, fruits, and other healthy foods can raise your body's defenses against stress and help you think more clearly in tough situations, other parts of your diet can decrease your ability to function under pressure. At the same time you're eating healthy foods, it's also important to cut down on unhelpful choices as much as possible.

Caffeine

Caffeine is a very common drug found in coffee, tea, soda, energy drinks, and many other beverages. It can also be "hidden" in some foods, including chocolate and ice cream—and even in aspirin, cold capsules, cough syrups, and other over-the-counter medicines.

Caffeine creates an artificial and temporary lift for people who are stressed-out and tired. It feels like energy, but it's very different from the kind you get from good food or physical activity. Like any mood-enhancing drug, the quick "up" creates the illusion that you're feeling better than you actually are.

Why can caffeine be a problem? Because it creates a physical reaction similar to the fight-or-flight response. Caffeine causes your body to release more of the stress hormone cortisol—essentially a bump in caffeine causes a bump in the stress you feel. A little can actually improve performance, but it's easy to overdo it. Instead of helping you feel on top of your game, caffeine can leave you feeling anxious and jittery. The drug can turn up the volume on your worries so that every moment you're looking over your shoulder for invisible tigers.

The side effects of too much caffeine are very similar to the symptoms of stress overload. Because of this, drinking caffeine is like drinking fear in small doses. Too much and you'll sense invisible tigers all around you. Unfortunately, caffeine can also be addictive and—like any addiction—the more you use it, the more it takes to produce the same effect. When you set out to eliminate or cut down on caffeine, you can experience some serious withdrawal symptoms, including major headaches. If you feel like you need a boost of energy and don't go for the caffeine, you may find yourself unconsciously drawn to another bad choice.

POSSIBLE SIDE EFFECTS OF CAFFEINE

- moodiness
- restlessness
- nervousness
- irritability
- shaking
- sleeplessness or nightmares
- sweaty hands or feet
- irregular heartbeat
- nervous or upset stomach
- intestinal disturbances
- panic attacks (sudden feelings of overwhelming anxiety that come without warning or any obvious reason)

Sugar

Like caffeine, sugar is also very common in our diets. It's often overlooked in foods because it can be listed under many different names—including glucose, sucrose, fructose, and corn syrup. These and other processed forms of sugar are chemically potent, and your body absorbs them quickly into the bloodstream. When this happens, your blood sugar rises quickly and can lead to a higher adrenaline level. This gives you an energy lift that lasts for about an hour before the effect wears off and you experience an energy crash. For this reason, large doses of sugar can generate mood swings where you feel up one moment and tired, stressed, or crabby the next.

What causes this up-down energy cycle? Simply put, the sudden boost in blood sugar surprises your pancreas. The average pancreas is generally a calm and stable organ. It maintains a normal level of sugar in the blood stream. You can imagine the excitement when all of a sudden—bam!—incoming sugar in mega-doses sets off an alarm. While you're getting the rush of sugar-driven energy, your pancreas jumps into high gear, secreting insulin to absorb the excess sugars and carry them off to the liver.

Sometimes, however, your pancreas puts out too much insulin and removes too much blood sugar, which can send you back into the sleepy head-nodding doldrums. You might begin to feel tired or cranky, and soon the vending machine is calling to you from down the hall. If you give in and buy another sugary drink or candy bar, you may find yourself strapped into the front seat of the Sugarcoaster. Up for a while, down again, and on and on. The problem is each down takes you deeper than the last, and by the end of a day, you're wiped out.

When the Sugarcoaster leaves you feeling low, a caffeine fix might seem like a good idea. But combining a lot of sugar and caffeine can be a prescription for exhaustion and confusion. One chemical (sugar) picks you up and later drops you off a cliff into a mild depressive state. The other (caffeine) strings you along with artificial energy that can give you headaches and cause you to exaggerate fears. While caffeine and sugar in moderate quantities usually do not lead to significant health problems, cutting down on them can definitely help you stay on top of stress.

SUGAR FIX

- The average person in the United States consumes about 225 pounds of sugar each year.
- Sugar has no vitamins, minerals, or nutritional value.
- Excess sugar is stored in your body as fat.
- One can of regular soda contains the equivalent of about half a sandwich bag full of white sugar.
- People in the United States drink over 50 million gallons of soda each year.
- Elevated soda consumption has been linked to increased risk of tooth decay, obesity, diabetes, and the bone disease osteoporosis.
- Sports drinks associated with health and fitness are often full of sugar.

Why It Can Be Hard to Eat Well

Unfortunately, many of us have very busy lives and don't make healthy eating a priority. Over the course of a stressful day, it can seem like there's no time for nutritious meals. Instead of finding food that's good for you, it's easier to stop at fast-food chains or convenience stores. It's not hard to find potato chips, candy bars, soda, or high-fat burgers and fries, but these on-the-go foods have very limited nutrients and often have ingredients that can be bad for your health.

Eating well is not always easy. Many schools are trying to give students healthier options, but some still have vending machines with sugary foods and sweet caffeinated drinks. It can also be extra hard for you to have a healthy diet if proper nutrition isn't a priority for your family, if good food is too expensive, or if you live in a neighborhood where good fruits and vegetables are hard to find.

Consider the hunt for healthy food to be a positive challenge. Arm yourself with information, then do your best to make good choices. Sometimes the best choice will mean avoiding unhealthy chemicals and other times it might mean ordering a salad at a fast-food restaurant instead of fried food. In addition to putting healthy fuel in your tank and consuming fewer stress-enhancing chemicals, eating right can boost your self-esteem. You can feel good knowing that you're treating your body right.

IMPORTANT!

All this talk about food, don't forget about the water! Did you know that water makes up 60 to 70 percent of our body weight? Most of our organs are made up of tissues with high water content, and maintaining that percentage is important toward our overall health. Blood is almost completely made up of water, and it serves many vital purposes—including maintaining a healthy body temperature, clearing the body of wastes, and ensuring organs receive important nutrients. That's why, in addition to a healthy diet, drinking enough water also is important. How much exactly do you need? Most experts believe eight to ten glasses a day will help keep your body functioning at a high level. (Of course, you may need more on days when you're very physically active.) If you have trouble drinking enough water, try to make it a point to have a glass every couple hours. Carry a water bottle with you and refill it as needed. Your body will thank you for it!

FIND OUT MORE

MyPlate.gov (myplate.gov). Visit this website to learn more about healthy eating options. You can enter your age, height, weight, and activity level to receive a tailor-made food plan for a healthy diet.

Center for Science in the Public Interest (cspinet.org/eating-healthy /ingredients-of-concern/caffeine-chart). The Center has a great website showing the caffeine content in foods and drinks.

Nutrition.gov (nutrition.gov). This website from the US Department of Agriculture is a one-stop source of information on getting essential nutrients from your diet, handling weight issues, planning for meals, and more. Look for links to information specifically for teens.

Topics to search online:
- How does caffeine affect my sleep?
- What is a caffeine withdrawal headache?
- What are some surprising foods or beverages that contain caffeine?
- What are other names for sugar?
- What foods contain hidden sugar?
- What are high school obesity rates by state or province? By country?
- Why should I drink so much water?

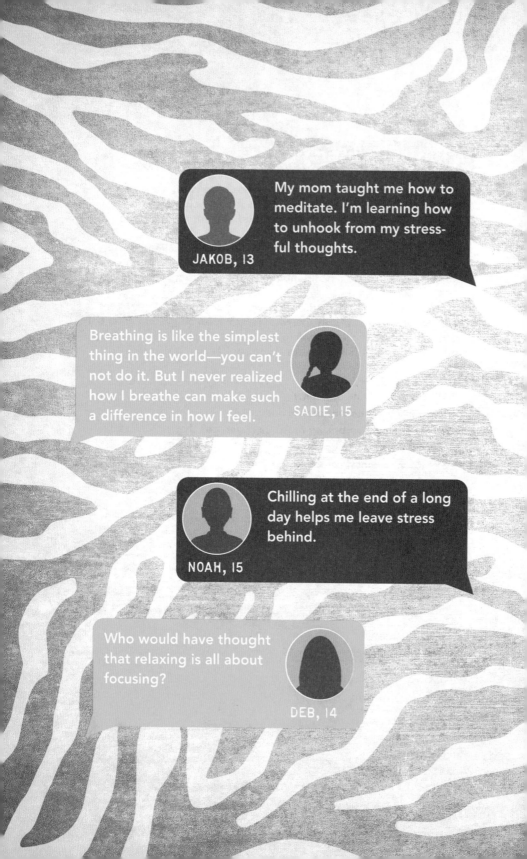

#3

FIND YOUR CALM CENTER

We all have moments when life seems overwhelming, when we feel uncertain or insecure. It's as if we're alone on a tiny lifeboat caught in a huge hurricane in the ocean. We get rocked by waves of emotion, tossed around by all the things we have to do, and almost blown over by our worries and fears. In those moments, it's natural to wonder if we can handle it, if we'll even survive.

When you're being tossed around in the stormy waves of life, another important set of stress management skills can help you find the eye of the hurricane—the calm place right in the middle of all the chaos, commotion, and confusion where you can rest up and recover. You don't have much control over the stressful storms of your life, but relaxation and mindfulness techniques can help you find that calm place.

What Are Relaxation and Mindfulness Techniques?

When you hear the word *relaxation*, you might think of playing video games or some other activity that gives you a break from the stressors in your life. But real relaxation and mindfulness techniques involve *non-doing.* Relaxation techniques enable you to be physically still while maintaining an alert but neutral mental focus. Some of the actions you might think of as "relaxing" may feel good, but they are coping behaviors—ways to avoid the feeling of being stressed. Real relaxation provides a form of deep rest for your body and mind and helps you feel relief from any invisible tigers chasing you.

The term *mindfulness* may be new to you. Mindfulness is a relaxation technique that emphasizes keeping your attention focused on something neutral, allowing you to remain centered in calm. It means ignoring physical sensations, thoughts of any kind, and what's going on in the world around you. When you are being mindful, your attention remains focused in a calm, neutral place. If your thoughts come to get you, you simply acknowledge them, let them go, and return to the calm center. One way to help stay focused is to concentrate on your breaths—in and out. This is known as mindful or focused breathing. You can learn more about this type of breathing on page 42.

Knowing how to relax and find your calm center helps keep your body and mind in tip-top, tiger-taming condition. Finding that calm place in the storm of stressors in your life is a skill, one that will take some practice.

Think about it. If you're always tense, your muscles never get a break. This constant tension can affect your entire body and lead to aches and pains. At some point you begin to feel tired all over and even start to lose flexibility so that simple, everyday activities seem harder and take more energy.

Similarly, constantly thinking or worrying about all the stressful situations in your life can lead to mental fatigue and exhaustion. Without the ability to relax and regroup in a calm place, you might begin to feel "brain fade"—that's when you lose some of your ability to think clearly and generate creative ideas. Relaxation skills can help you pull yourself back together so you can feel calm and capable.

COPING OR REAL RELAXATION?

Can you spot the true relaxation techniques in this list?
1. Streaming funny videos
2. Going for a walk
3. Focusing on your breathing
4. Taking a nap
5. Gradually tensing and relaxing your muscles
6. Reading a book
7. Meditating
8. Chatting with a friend online

If you guessed 3, 5, and 7 are the relaxation techniques, you're right. Everything else, no matter how pleasant, falls in the category of coping strategies. While watching TV, reading, and chatting online can all be fun and give you a break from the hard stuff, they're not relaxation techniques because your brain is busy and your mental focus isn't neutral. Going for a walk can be a nice break, but it's not a relaxation exercise because you're not physically still, you have to watch out for traffic, and your mind can easily wander into worrying. Sleeping isn't a relaxation technique either because it isn't a controlled state and you're not alert. Nightmares are proof that sleep isn't always relaxing.

Coping strategies make you feel better temporarily because they mask or distract you from anxiety and tension. But the only real relaxation techniques on the list are focused breathing, meditation, and muscle relaxation—techniques where you are calm, alert, and have a neutral mental focus.

BRAIN WAVES

The billions of cells in your brain use electricity to communicate. This electrical communication can be measured by high-tech sensors and shows up as visible wave forms on a monitor. Your brain has different wave patterns, depending on whether you're stressed, calm, or asleep. Researchers have shown that relaxation exercises promote an alpha brain wave pattern—a pattern that shows a state of alertness and physical and mental relaxation.

Focused Breathing

Your body and mind influence one another in powerful ways. Your thoughts and feelings affect your body chemistry. At the same time, how you feel physically influences your attitude and mood. Bringing body and mind into balance with each other helps you be more relaxed, rested, and in control of how you're feeling. Focused breathing is an easy way to create calmness in the center of a stress-filled day.

When you're nervous, excited, or angry, your breathing is more rapid and tends to move up in your chest. The result is short, shallow breaths that don't provide your body with the oxygen it needs. When you're relaxed and at ease, on the other hand, your breathing is slower and deeper. **Slow, deep, regular breathing is the physical expression of a calm mind.**

What is your breathing like right now? Because you're sitting down and reading a book, your breathing is probably deep and slow. The next time you're feeling stressed, check your breath. It will most likely be a lot faster and shallower. Just sitting and worrying about something (or *many* things) can change your breathing. The good news is you can learn to control your breathing to achieve a calmer mental state—even during times of high stress. The following exercise can help you learn how.

IMPORTANT!

Until you master the steps of the exercises in this section, you might want to have someone read them to you. For example, you and a friend could take turns reading and relaxing. You can also find MP3 files of the relaxation scripts at freespirit.com. Search for *Fighting Invisible Tigers* to find files you can download to your phone or other device.

Getting Ready

- Find an appropriate location to perform this exercise. You'll need a comfortable place to lie down where it's quiet and you're not likely to be disturbed.
- Loosen any tight clothing or belts that might restrict your breathing. You may also wish to remove your shoes for comfort.
- Commit to doing the Focused Breathing exercise until it's over. Stopping early won't allow you to get the full benefit.
- You may want to tell the people around you what you're doing—you don't want them to panic if they walk in and see you laying on the floor and not moving!
- Cycle through all the steps of the exercise three to four times. Your breathing should deepen and slow so that you feel calmer. Allow your breathing to quicken to its normal rate before getting up.

Focused Breathing Exercise

1. Sit up straight or lie in a comfortable position.
2. Keeping your mouth closed, inhale and exhale deeply through your nose a few times to settle into the moment.
3. Place your right hand on your stomach, near your belly button, and your left hand at the top of your chest.

4. Do not try to control your breathing yet. Just notice where in your body your breath is located.

5. Take a long, slow, deep breath into your chest. Your left hand should rise with the inhalation, but your right hand should remain pretty still.

6. Pause briefly, keeping your chest full, and then release and allow a slow exhale through your nose.

7. Repeat this chest breathing three times. Breathe in, chest rises . . . hold . . . release and exhale.
  • Notice which muscles are involved, the sensation of fullness at the pause, and the feeling of relaxation that comes with the slow, deliberate release of air.
  • In . . . hold . . . release.
  • In . . . hold . . . release.

8. Take a break. Stop controlling your breath for a few rounds and wait till your breathing finds its own rhythm and natural location.

9. Again take a long, slow, deep breath, but this time, direct the inhalation into the bottom of your diaphragm (just below your rib cage), hold, and release. Your right hand near your belly button should rise and fall while your left hand stays pretty still.

10. Repeat this belly breathing three times.
  • Breathe in, right hand rises . . . hold . . . release.
  • In . . . hold . . . release.
  • In . . . hold . . . release.

11. When you're done, take another break and give your breathing a chance to return to its natural state.

12. Now, keeping both your hands in place, combine all the breathing movements into one slow, continuous, four-count exercise, like this:
  • Count "one" and breathe into your belly so your right hand rises. Pause for a mini-second.

- Count "two" and breathe into your chest so your left hand rises. Pause for a mini-second.
- Count "three" and begin a controlled, gradual exhalation from your belly so your right hand lowers. Pause for a mini-second.
- Count "four" and slowly release the remaining air in your chest so your left hand lowers.

13. When you feel you have completely exhaled, pause for a split-second before you start the cycle again.

14. Repeat this four-count breathing pattern for two to three minutes. You can say this rhythmic chant to yourself: inhale belly, inhale chest, exhale belly, exhale chest.

Focusing on your breathing and counting like this may be difficult or feel strange at first, but with a little practice, the activity can feel natural and very soothing. As you get more comfortable with the exercise, you may want to lengthen your sessions. Once you're familiar with this way of creating the peaceful eye in the center of the storm, you'll be able to visit the calm place whenever you're beginning to feel overwhelmed with stress.

BREATHE IN   HOLD   RELEASE

Sitting in the Calm

Just as your heart beats endlessly and automatically day in and day out, your mind is "always on"—it's a thinking machine that produces an endless stream of thoughts. If you don't believe it, here's an experiment to prove it: Set down this book for a moment, close your eyes, and turn off your brain. Ready? Stop thinking right . . . now!

Did it work? Of course not. Shutting off your brain is simply impossible. No matter what you do, your thoughts continually lurk in the background. This includes your fears and worries—your own thoughts can become some of your worst invisible tigers.

Although you can't stop the flow of your thoughts, you can learn how to detach from them and focus your attention on something else. For example, right now, move your attention to the bottom of your right foot. Did you suddenly become more aware of what was going on there? Now, shift your attention to the sensation of your hand holding this book. There it is. You can suddenly feel the book even though you weren't noticing it before.

The attention rule goes like this: What we pay attention to gets louder or more prominent in the moment. The same is true for our thoughts. Sometimes we're thinking about what's outside of us, and other times we're busy with our inner thoughts. Our thoughts shift fairly easily, but wherever our focus lands, that's what commands our attention.

The primary challenges of relaxation, mindfulness, and meditation skills are learning to be physically still, focusing your attention on something other than your thoughts, and then keeping it there. This meditation exercise can help you learn to detach from your thinking machine and simply sit in calm.

Getting Ready

- Choose a time and place you're likely not to be disturbed. Remember to turn off your cell phone and eliminate other possible distractions.

- Commit to the exercise. Decide before you start how long the session will last. In the beginning, three to five minutes is enough. Later, you may want to lengthen your sessions. Whatever length you choose, set a timer and don't stop until time is up.

- During the activity, don't control your breathing. Let your breathing find a depth and rhythm that's naturally comfortable.

- Don't move. You should keep your body still for the entire session. If you focus your attention on what your body is doing or feeling, you will become distracted from the experience.

Sitting in Calm Exercise

1. Place a firm chair in front of a blank wall.

2. Sit on the chair facing the wall with your back relaxed but straight. This position may feel uncomfortable at first, but it will become more comfortable over time.

3. Put your feet flat on the floor.

4. Fold your hands in your lap or place them palms-down on top of your thighs.

5. Keep your head up and pull your chin in a little to keep your neck straight.

6. Keep your eyes open but look down at about a 45-degree angle at the blank wall. Don't tilt your head—just look down.

7. When you have the position right, focus on your breathing. Don't try to control it in any way—just keep your mouth closed and give your attention to the passing of the inhalations and exhalations through your nose.

8. When you're ready to begin, silently count "one" on the next inhalation and "two" on the exhalation, "three" on the next inhalation and "four" on the exhalation . . . and so on up to "ten." When you reach "ten," start over with "one" on the next inhale.

Roadblocks to Sitting in Calm

When you set out to sit still in calm, many distractions can come up. Here are some you might encounter and instructions for dealing with them.

Roadblock #1: Your Rebellious Mind. Your mind may not appreciate your attempts to control your focus of attention. It's used to being in charge, driving the bus, going where it wants, and keeping you busy with thinking, worrying, and planning. Just as you settle into the comfort of counting breaths, your mind will start sending distracting thoughts to get back in charge. Before you know it, you can be lost in thought and forget you were even counting.

Roadblock #2: Your Rebellious Body. Just like your mind, your body may not be used to sitting absolutely still and will do its best to distract you. As you sit in calm, some parts may twitch, tingle, or go numb. You might feel itchy, hungry, thirsty, achy . . . *if* you allow yourself to focus on these sensations. Remember, the body and mind influence each other. All bodily distractions are simply the expression of a restless mind. No matter how compelling a physical sensation may seem, it will go away if you cease to magnify it with your attention.

Roadblock #3: The World. Somehow the whole world seems to know when you're about to sit down for a moment of mindfulness. Friends stop by or your phone vibrates, people knock on your door, your little brother barges into the room, or the next-door neighbor picks this moment to mow the lawn.

Getting Around Roadblocks. If you are distracted by your mind, your body, or the world, return your attention to your breathing and focus on counting. Begin at "one" on the next inhalation and continue counting again. The first few times you try meditating, you may start over a lot. That's okay. With practice, you can improve your ability to stay focused on your breathing and detaching from your mind and body.

Progressive Muscle Relaxation (PMR)

When stressed people talk about being "uptight" or "tense," they're not just describing how they feel but also the condition of their muscles. In the early 1900s, Dr. Edmund Jacobson learned that muscles could be deeply relaxed by intentionally holding and then releasing tension. Dr. Jacobson called this exercise progressive relaxation. Today it's referred to as progressive muscle relaxation or PMR.

PMR is easy to do. You isolate different muscle groups and systematically tighten and release them. By developing a routine and practicing it regularly, you'll soon have another approach to finding your calm center.

One benefit of PMR is that you don't have to be alone in a quiet place to do it. You may want to learn in a safe and private setting, but once you become skilled at the technique, you can do it anytime or anywhere you like.

Getting Ready

- Wear comfortable clothing. Tight clothing or belts applying pressure to your body can cause you to be uncomfortable and make it difficult to concentrate. You may also wish to remove your shoes.

- Find a comfortable place to sit or lie down where it's quiet and you're not likely to be disturbed.

- While there is no risk of injury during PMR, be cautious about any muscles that have recently been injured or are prone to cramping.

- Take natural, relaxed breaths as you do the exercise, and keep your focus on what is happening in your muscles. Feel the buildup and release of tension in each particular muscle group. It is often helpful to visualize the particular muscle group being tensed and then released.

- When you are holding tension in one part of your body, make sure other parts stay relaxed. Only tense the part you're training.

- As you go through the PMR exercise, it's important to notice the difference between tense and relaxed muscles.

Progressive Muscle Relaxation (PMR) Exercise

1. Lie on a flat surface. Begin your PMR session by tensing the muscles in your feet. Bend your toes down and hold them for three to five seconds. You may want to count to yourself saying one thousand one, one thousand two . . . up to five. Then quickly release the tension. Next, pull your toes up and again hold that position as tight as you can for three to five seconds. Again, quickly relax your feet. Notice the sensation of release and the absence of tension.

2. Next, tighten all the muscles from your feet up to your waist. Start with tightening your calf muscles, then tighten your thighs, and finally squeeze your buttocks. Check to see that your feet and everything above your waist is relaxed. Hold them all as tightly as you can for three to five seconds . . . and then quickly release. Again, take a moment to notice the sensation of release and how it feels to have the tension drain away.

3. Now repeat this procedure with the muscles in your stomach. Tighten and hold the tension for three to five seconds, and then release and pause to notice the feeling.

4. Moving up to your chest—tighten those muscles and hold the tension for three to five seconds . . . and then release. Release your breath.

5. Now tense the muscles in your shoulders by lifting and holding them for three to five seconds. Make sure to have all the surrounding muscles relaxed and keep the tension in the area of your shoulders. Then release the muscles in your shoulders and feel them sinking back onto the floor.

6. Tighten just your hands by forming fists. Hold them tightly for three to five seconds and release the effort and tension.

7. Tighten your hands by bending them back at the wrist. Continue to build the tension in your forearms, biceps, and triceps. Hold this position for three to five seconds and release and let the muscles soften and relax.

8. Tense your neck by turning your head as far as you can to the right and holding it for three to five seconds. Then turn your

head back to center and relax. Now turn it to the left as far as you can and hold that position for three to five seconds. Again, return to center and release the effort. Feel the weight of your head on the floor.

9. Next, contract the muscles in your face. Press your lips together, wrinkle your nose, tighten your forehead, and squeeze your eyes shut. Hold this position for three to five seconds, and then quickly let the tension drain away and feel your face returning to its normal position.

10. Finally, do a quick scan of your whole body for any remaining tension. Imagine a wave of relaxation starting at your toes, moving up your body, moving up your arms, and sweeping any remaining tension right out the top of your head. Enjoy the feeling of deep muscle relaxation and whole-body calm.

11. When you're ready, take a couple of slow, deep breaths, open your eyes, put a smile on your face, then sit up and head back into your life . . . refreshed.

This may seem like a lot to do, but once you've been through it a few times, it goes fairly quickly. The whole activity, tensing and releasing each part of your body and pausing to feel the sensations of relaxation in between, can be done in 10 to 15 minutes. When you're finished, your body will feel very heavy and calm with the tension released. Your breathing and heart rate will have slowed down, and your mind will be more likely to enter into a relaxed state. Learning PMR is great because it allows you to have greater awareness of your body and release tension in the moment you experience it.

Will relaxation and mindfulness skills eliminate all stress from your life or make your wildest dreams come true? Probably not. But they can help you feel less overwhelmed, worried, or insecure. Real relaxation takes you directly to the calm place in the center of the stress storm and enables you to experience deep physical release and mental calm. The more you practice relaxation skills, the more capable you become at staying centered in calm—throughout a regular day as well as when you're surrounded by invisible tigers.

FIND OUT MORE

KidsHealth: Relaxation Exercises (kidshealth.org/en/teens /relax-breathing.html). This site has some great meditation audios and exercises.

Mindfulness for Teens (mindfulnessforteens.com). This site offers a wide variety of guided meditations and mindfulness tips.

Topics to search online:
- What brain wave patterns are associated with deep relaxation?
- How does progressive muscle relaxation calm the mind?
- What is selective attention?
- How long have people been meditating?
- What are some good deep breathing exercises?

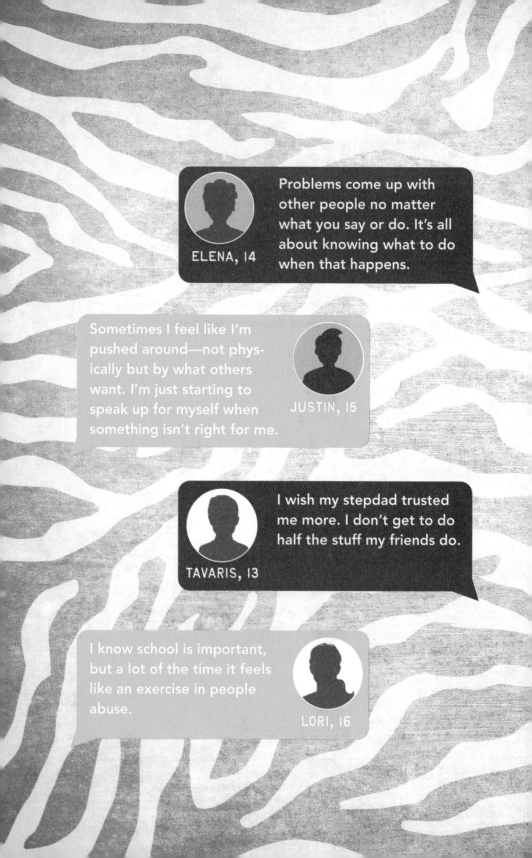

#4

STAND UP FOR YOURSELF

A lot of the stress we feel comes from how well we get along with others. For example, at times, you may feel disrespected by your friends or that other people—including family adults, teachers, or other adults—have too much control over your life. Maybe you sometimes feel like your needs, opinions, and feelings don't count, that everything is decided for you. Or maybe you feel like your family and school responsibilities take up a lot of your free time. And when you do have time for yourself, maybe limits are placed on what you can do or how much time you spend doing the activities you enjoy. Assertiveness skills can help you with the stress caused by these kinds of situations.

Assertiveness Skills

Others may have a lot to say about some parts of your life, but you actually have more control than you might realize. Some rules at school or home don't seem fair, but you probably know from experience that rebelling against them doesn't usually help. Assertiveness skills can help you stand up for yourself in positive ways.

ASSERTIVENESS QUIZ

1. If teachers are unfair, do you talk to them about it?
2. If you know a friend lies to you, do you say something?
3. If a person sends nasty text messages or posts negative things about you, do you talk with someone about it?
4. If you're waiting in line and someone cuts in front of you, do you speak up?
5. Do you confront people who try to embarrass or gossip about you in person or online?
6. If a friend wants you to do something you're not comfortable with, can you say "no"?
7. Can you discuss household rules (like curfew or chores) without arguing?
8. If someone is bullying you at school or online, are you able to tell an adult?
9. Are you able to tell your friends the truth about what you think and who you are?
10. Are you able to resolve conflicts with others without getting angry and aggressive?

If you answered no to some or most of these questions, you could benefit from a boost in assertiveness. Assertiveness skills help you honestly share your thoughts and feelings without disrespecting others. They help you set limits on what is and isn't okay with you and ask for what you want and need. When you're assertive, people know who you are and what you think and feel, and they understand your ground rules for relationships. Assertiveness can help you protect the rights you have as a person.

Your Basic Rights

- You have the right to have your feelings, needs, and opinions heard and considered.

- You have the right to have input into the decisions that affect your life.

- You have the right to say, "No," "I don't know," "I don't under-stand," or "I'm not interested in doing that."

- You have the right to stand up to people who threaten, tease, or put you down.

- You have the right to share your feelings.

- You have the right to be different and celebrate your uniqueness.

- You have the right to like yourself even when you're less than perfect.

- You have the right to respond to violations of your rights.

These rights also come with responsibilities. For example, you don't have the right to share your feelings about others by putting them down or physically hurting them—assertiveness is not the same as aggressiveness. When you're being aggressive, you don't consider others' feelings, and it can cost you respect and drive people away. When you're assertive, on the other hand, you can handle challenges in ways that are respectful and recognize others' feelings.

The ASSERT Formula

You might know from experience that keeping a level head when you feel you've been wronged can be difficult. Tough situations can come up and make it hard to keep your cool. Other times you might feel afraid to speak up about something that's bothering you. Assertiveness skills come in handy in all these situations.

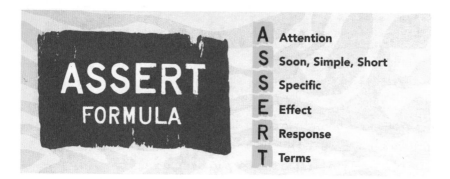

Attention. To work on problems you're having with others, you first have to get their **attention**. Engage the person in a respectful way and tell him or her you want to talk about something important.

Soon, Simple, Short. Respond as **soon** as possible to a situation. Letting something go unaddressed can cause you stress for a long time. If you're upset and afraid you might react in a negative or harmful way, talk to the person as soon as you've calmed down. When you are ready to discuss the issue, keep your explanation of the problem **simple** and **short**.

Specific. When you're describing the situation, focus on the **specific** behavior—what a person has said or done—that's causing you to be uncomfortable.

Effect. Help others understand the **effect** a situation is having on you. Share with the other person how the specific behavior causes you to feel.

Response. Describe the **response** you would like from him or her that would help resolve the issue. Then ask the other person for feedback on your request.

Terms. Finally, after discussing the specific behavior and your request for change, briefly restate the **terms** of your mutual agreement to make sure everything is clear.

Here are three examples of how and when to use the ASSERT formula to give you an idea of what it will sound like when you put it into action.

SITUATION #1

There's a scuffle near you in the hall at school. Some teachers break it up and take away the students who were fighting. One of the teachers takes you to the office. You try to explain you weren't involved in the fight, but the teacher isn't listening.

Attention: "Mrs. Williams, can I talk to you about what just happened?"

Soon, Simple, Short: "I wasn't involved in the fight in any way, and I feel it's unfair for me to be punished."

Specific: "I understand that you thought I was involved, and I can see how you made the mistake. But I was only walking by when the fight began."

Effect: "I'm upset because I don't want to be suspended and miss school for something I didn't do. I also feel hurt that you believe I'd even think of fighting in school."

Response: "Would you be willing to listen to my side of the story? I was close to the situation and can tell you what I saw."

Terms: "Thanks. I really appreciate knowing that you're willing to hear me out."

SITUATION #2

Your mom yells at you to get off the phone when you're talking with friends. Your friends can hear her, and the shouting embarrasses you.

Attention: "Mom, can we take a second to talk about what just happened while I was on the phone? This is very important to me."

Soon, Simple, Short: "I'm having a problem with how you let me know when you want me to get off the phone."

Specific: "I don't like being yelled at when you feel I've been on the phone too long."

Effect on Me: "When you do that, my friends hear you and I'm embarrassed."

Response: "Would you be willing to try something different? If you held up two fingers to let me know I have two minutes to get off the phone, it would give me enough time to finish my conversation. I think it would be easier on both of us."

Terms: "Okay, so you'll hold up two fingers instead of yelling, and I'll get off the phone within two minutes. Thanks for being willing to try this idea."

SITUATION #3

A longtime friend from the neighborhood has joined the football team and now mostly hangs out with other players at school. If your friend sees you when he's with the team, he ignores you. You haven't hung out together in a few weeks.

Attention: "Hey, Jake. Do you have a minute to talk about something that's bothering me?"

Soon, Simple, Short: "Ever since you joined the football team, it seems like you don't have time for our friendship."

Specific: "It seems like you only spend time with other players, and when I do see you, you ignore me. We hardly hang out anymore."

Effect: "It's cool that you're on the football team, and I understand you need to have other friends. But I feel hurt because we've been close for a long time and now it seems like you don't want to spend time with me."

Response: "I would still like to hang out with you once in a while. Maybe we could get together at a time when you don't have practice."

Terms: "Thanks. I really appreciate knowing you still care about our friendship and that you want to spend time together. See you Sunday!"

(If Jake doesn't have time to hang out with you, it might be time to build other friendships. "Weave a Safety Net of Support" on pages 65–73 has some ideas for expanding your social circle.)

The ASSERT formula may feel mechanical and awkward at first, but with practice it can become more natural. Even though it's a simple formula, it can be quite powerful. When you are assertive with others about what you want to happen, you are more likely to get your needs met as well as get more respect. While you may not always get what you want, at least you've explained how you feel and tried to make the situation better. Using this form of assertiveness is like saying, "I'm taking this risk because I care about our relationship and I want it to work for both of us." That kind of statement can go a long way toward how people see and treat you in the future.

Expressing your feelings in positive and assertive ways is like having a safety valve that allows you to release the pressure of strong negative feelings and keeps you from reaching the bursting point. It can also help you understand yourself better, feel less vulnerable, and get more of what you want and deserve in life. That's much better than heading out into a jungle full of threatening stress tigers without any defenses.

IMPORTANT!

It's important to use your judgment when using the ASSERT formula. For example, you don't want to provoke someone who is violent, abusive, or under the influence of drugs or alcohol. These skills work best when you're dealing with a person who is reasonable and ready and willing to hear your side of an issue. If you ever feel your safety is in danger, get away from the situation and find help right away.

FIND OUT MORE

Above the Influence (abovetheinfluence.com). A program from the nonprofit Partnership for Drug-Free Kids, the Above the Influence website is a resource for teens looking to move beyond peer pressure and stand up for their values and beliefs. The site features games, videos, quizzes, student stories, and suggestions for staying assertive when others try to make decisions for you.

Stick Up for Yourself! Every Kid's Guide to Personal Power and Positive Self-Esteem by Gershen Kaufman and Lev Raphael. This book provides real-life scenarios and personal power tools you can use to stand firm when others want to push you around. Find out what to say in tough situations, ideas for ending conflicts, and much more.

Topics to search online:
- How is assertive behavior different from being aggressive?
- What are the benefits of being assertive?
- Show me a video of how to be assertive.
- What does it mean to be passive-aggressive?

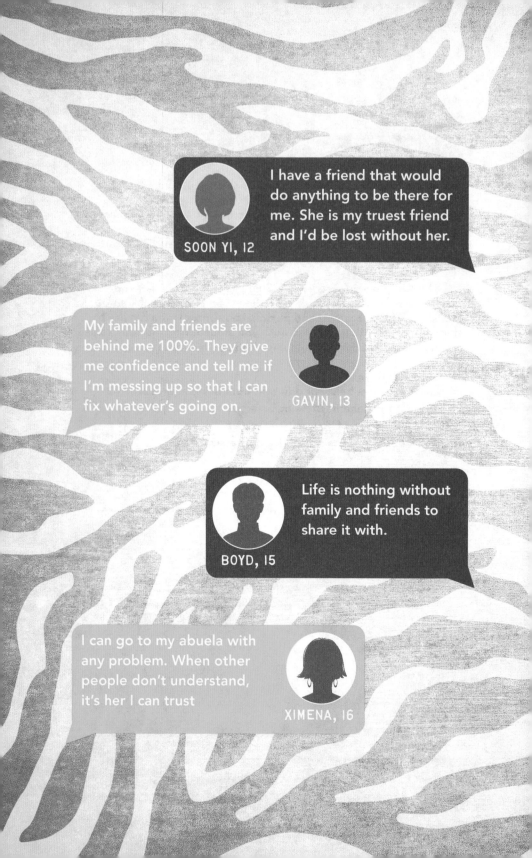

WEAVE A SAFETY NET OF SUPPORT

Have you ever felt stressed about something but kept the problem to yourself? Maybe you didn't want to worry anyone or you were afraid others would look down on you. It's natural to want to appear capable, strong, and able to get through tough times. But sometimes the fear of showing uncertainty or vulnerability can lead us to close ourselves off when we're most in need of support. It's during hard or stressful times that a safety net of trusted people can be especially helpful.

The Importance of Weaving a Safety Net

Sometimes it can feel like we're supposed to be superheroes—to handle all the challenges in life alone, and if we can't, then something is wrong with us. It also can seem like we should be able to do new things on our own, even if we've never done them before. Unfortunately, these thoughts have the power to make us feel bad about ourselves and think we're alone in dealing with the stressful parts of life.

- Do you feel the need to put up a front or try to impress others?

- Do you ever say you're doing fine—even when you're not feeling well?

- Do you feel like you have to sometimes lie about what you like or who you are?

- Do you wonder if you can truly trust people for support when you're in a crisis?

- Do you feel you have to "go it alone" when you're overwhelmed, frightened, or confused?

HEALING FRIENDS
Friendships, family support, and other trusted adults are so important that they actually affect your physical health. Studies show that spending time and talking with caring friends and family members reduces the presence of cortisol and other stress hormones that delay healing. Connecting with others even has benefits at the cellular level!

The truth is, family, good friends, and other supportive and caring adults are important sources of help for staying on top of stress and dealing with challenges. Together, these people form a safety net, much like the net under high-wire performers at a circus. Knowing they are there for you can give you the courage to face problems and try new things. When you're out there taking a risk, teetering on the wire, it's great to know you're not alone and there's a group of trustworthy people who will catch you if you fall.

Human safety nets don't simply appear when you need them. Instead they have to be intentionally created and strengthened over time. You can start by being a supportive person yourself. Being there for friends or family members when they're down or need help allows you to build trust. When you show you can be counted on, others are more likely to be there for you.

The Five Levels of Relationships

Think for a moment about the people you know. Are there some people you really trust and go to for help if you need it—like family members or best friends? Are there others you know but aren't especially close to? If you think about it, you probably have all kinds of different relationships—from people you can't live without to people you find it hard to live with.

If you had to grade your relationships, you might start by thinking about how much you trust them. A trust scale might look like this:

One way to gauge the amount of trust in a relationship is to think about the things you talk about with other people. What do you share with friends and family members? What do these people share with you? As you read the following descriptions, think about the people you know and which categories they might fit into.

Level 1—"Just the facts . . ."

In level 1 relationships, facts are shared. A lot of everyday conversation between acquaintances is spent at level 1. It's nonthreatening, because the subject matter isn't about the people doing the talking or anything really controversial.

"There's a basketball game on Saturday night."

"We're having a history test on chapter 4 this Friday."

"I dropped my phone and the screen broke again!"

Level 2—"They say . . ."

Level 2 relationships are also pretty safe territory because conversations are about what other people have said. The risk of offending someone or being rejected because of what's said is pretty low because you don't say what you are thinking or feeling. Instead, you're like a reporter sharing what you've heard, read, or seen somewhere else. Unfortunately, a lot of level 2 talk can be gossip or put-downs toward others.

"I hear Brooklynne has a new boyfriend and he's just using her."

"They say the math teacher is tough."

"Paulo told me the team got crushed at the game last night."

Level 3—"I think . . ."

Level 3 conversations are where real connections between people begin. Some trust is required at this level because you are taking a risk by revealing your opinions and ideas. There's the possibility of anger, arguments, or hurt feelings, but also the opportunity to build solid friendships based on things you share.

"That song is awesome."

"I think using drugs is stupid."

"We should have a say in how our school is run."

Level 4—"I feel . . ."

In level 4 conversations, feelings are shared and genuine emotions are expressed. For example, a friend upset about a breakup wouldn't be afraid to cry or show feelings in front of you. At the same time, you would try to understand your friend's feelings and provide comfort. Level 4 conversations require trust because people can feel vulnerable and need to be confident of your support before opening up. This isn't the kind of exchange that goes well online; it is best done in person. This is where real connections between people takes place and solid friendships are formed.

> **"My parents are getting divorced. I feel afraid and angry that they'd break up our family."**

> **"It makes me happy that my mom got the job she's always wanted."**

> **"I'm so upset about my math grade I could scream."**

Level 5—"This is how I feel about you."

Level 5 is an extension of level 4. At this level, you directly share your feelings for or about another person. This includes feelings of love, hurt, frustration, happiness, or whatever else is going on between you. While these conversations can be hard, they also can make relationships stronger. Think of a time when you and a parent argued but talked things over and came to an agreement. It's possible you felt closer after working things out. Level 5 relationships involve the greatest risk because you're the most vulnerable and require the most trust.

> **"I appreciate how you stood up for me. You really are a good friend, and I feel lucky to know you."**

> **"It makes me sad that you're moving. I don't want to lose your friendship."**

> **"I'm worried because you've seemed depressed for days, and the way you're acting scares me."**

Here's what happens when we add this new information to the Trust Scale:

Low Trust		Medium Trust		High Trust
1	**2**	**3**	**4**	**5**
Just the facts . . .	They say . . .	I think . . .	I feel . . .	I feel . . . about us

TRUST SCALE

Now that you're familiar with the Trust Scale and the five levels of relationships, you can rate your own support system. Include family members, neighbors, friends, teachers, counselors, and other people at school or in your community.

TRUST SCALE

Low Trust		Medium Trust		High Trust
1	**2**	**3**	**4**	**5**
Just the facts . . .	They say . . .	I think . . .	I feel . . .	I feel . . . about us
Randy	Abigail	LaTisha	Coach Ken	Dad
Erin	Nora	Mr. Jacobsen	Ms. Lee	Mom
Brittany	Claudia	Mrs. Sampson	Rabbi Green	McKenzie
Aman	Kirsten	Will	Maria	Aunt Sally
Ai	Mary			Nana
Santana	Alex			

When you're done, you'll have a basic map of your relationships. You may have many 1s, 2s, and 3s but need to build some stronger 4 or 5 connections. Or, you might only have a couple people you're very close to. Whatever it looks like now, the map can tell you about the quality of your current safety net and help you identify relationships you'd like to make stronger.

Your goal doesn't have to be to turn all your relationships into 5s—everyone also needs 1s, 2s, 3s, and 4s in their lives. These are people who can be fun to hang out with, teach you cool things, offer different perspectives, and introduce you to new experiences. While it's not essential to be extremely close with everyone you know, weaving a strong safety net does mean developing a few 4s and 5s in your life for support when you need it. Knowing you have people you can trust and count on keeps you from facing the invisible tigers of life on your own.

Strengthening Relationships

What can you do if you want to make your relationships with friends, family, and others stronger? Do you go up to someone and say: "Hey, we're about a 2 on the relationship scale. I'd like to see us reach level 4 or 5—do you want to discuss your deep feelings with me?" You could say this, but there's a good chance the other person would look at you like you're crazy—and then maybe run away. The good news: You can try many other less awkward ways to strengthen relationships.

Spend time together. This may sound obvious, but activities with friends and family provide some of the best bonding experiences. No matter what you're doing, interesting or funny things are likely to happen that give you something to talk or laugh about together. Joining sports or drama, going to the skateboard park, hanging in the gym, or other fun activities are great ways to connect with others. As you spend time together and share interests, you'll have experiences that can bring you closer.

Be honest. When it comes to improving relationships, honesty is always the best policy. Lying to parents, teachers, or other adults results in distrust that damages relationships. The same is true for friendships. Lying to or about others is irresponsible and disrespectful. It can cause fallouts that are difficult to repair. The next time you feel the need to stretch the truth, remember that lies nearly always come back to hurt (or even destroy) relationships. Telling the truth, especially when it's hard, is how you earn level 4 and 5 relationships.

Take an interest in things that are important to others. Being genuinely interested in what people like or enjoy is a kind of compliment. It shows you care about them. Most people enjoy talking about the activities in their lives, and the good feeling they have discussing these things can rub off on you.

Don't pressure others. Bossy people generally don't make very good friends. Do you want to hang around someone who constantly tells you what to do or tries to make you do things that you're uncomfortable with? Probably not. If you feel the urge to pressure people or tell them what to do or think, try to stop yourself by remembering how it would feel coming back at you. Real friends give each other permission to be themselves.

Avoid overemphasizing yourself. It's good to share information about yourself with others—talking about your thoughts, feelings, and interests is a good way to establish common ground. At the same time, sharing can be overdone. You might know a few people who think the world revolves around them, they're doing the best things, and you're dying to hear all about their lives. Braggarts, or "center of the universe" people, usually do a pretty good job of turning others off. It's good to share, but it's also important to listen to what others have to say. In good friendships most aspects of the relationship are shared equally.

Offer your help. When you think someone could use a hand, offer it. Whether it's pitching in on chores at home or taking time to explain a math assignment to a classmate, make your move. Good deeds usually generate gratitude and good feelings—it's hard for people not to like someone who wants to help. The same holds true for difficult situations where you know even a quick chat or word of encouragement could do someone a world of good. You may not even be that close, but a gesture that says you understand how he or she is feeling shows your potential to become a close friend.

Ask for support. Asking someone for help means you trust a person enough to lean on them when you need to. It also means you're smart enough to know you're at the limits of what you can handle. When you turn to your safety net for help, your relationships with those people can get even stronger.

FIND OUT MORE

How Rude! The Teen Guide to Good Manners, Proper Behavior, and Not Grossing People Out by Alex J. Packer. Getting along with others begins with politeness. This book has the lowdown on giving and getting respect.

The InSite (theinsite.org). Visit this site for information on dealing with the ups and downs of relationships—including friendship troubles, family spats, and rough spots with teachers and other adults.

Teen Central (teencentral.com). Teen Central features real stories about relationships and other issues. You also can submit your own questions and get feedback from others.

Topics to search online:
- What do I do when a good friend lets me down?
- How do I make my friendships stronger?
- What's the best way to make good friends?
- What are the traits of a great best friend?

I know where I'm going—even in the hard times I keep my eyes on the prize.

MING, 15

Life is so much easier when you have an idea of what's going to happen next.

ASHA, 17

If you don't make sure you're on the right path, who will?

RONALD, 13

Goals give you more power over your own destiny.

INGRID, 14

I'll be happy to graduate. I like to weld, so I may go to body shop school or learn heating and air conditioning.

DANNY, 17

#6
TAKE CHARGE
OF YOUR LIFE

Do you ever feel like you're not in charge of your life? Like you're doing the best you can but things just happen to you without your control? Maybe you feel so stressed that right now all you can do is keep up, let alone think about what you want to do in the future. Feeling this way can make it seem like your life is a movie—one where you're only a character following directions from someone else calling the shots.

Not feeling in control of the action or being confused about how your movie should play out can cause a lot of stress. If you're not moving toward what you want, goals can help you get back in the director's chair. It is your life after all—why not make it great?

Writing Your Own Script

How can you get back in the director's chair? Ask yourself some important, big questions, the ones that have the power to shape your future: "Where is my life heading? Why am I going in this direction? Who decided? What's really important to me? What do I want to be working toward? What difference do I want to make in the world?"

These life questions can be difficult to answer—so difficult that many people avoid thinking about them at all. But charging through life without a sense of direction or purpose can leave you feeling like you're running in place. You can start taking charge by writing a script for a movie called *My Life*.

To start writing your script, think about the things you would like to accomplish. These might be goals you have for the immediate future (such as getting a summer job or making the swim team) or longer-term achievements you'd like to work toward (like graduating with good grades). No matter how big or small accomplishments might seem, setting goals helps you achieve them. And, you can reduce stress because you're working toward a life you want.

Goal Questions

If you're having trouble coming up with goals, use these questions to get you thinking in the right direction.

1. **What are your interests or special talents?** People are happiest when they're doing what they love or are good at. Try to imagine goals related to your interests, passions, and abilities.

2. **What would you most like to be known for?** When we're respected for our accomplishments, we're more likely to be happy. Think of achievements you might like to be known for.

3. **What's most important to you?** Doing things that are person-ally meaningful help us feel balanced and satisfied. Think of goals that would make you feel good about yourself.

4. **Who are your heroes?** The people we admire offer us a window into our own dreams. Think of your heroes—people you look up to who have made a difference in the world—and why they stand out to you. In what ways would you like their strengths and accomplishments to be reflected in yours?

5. **Where do you want to live?** Where we live can play a big role in the opportunities available to us. Try to imagine your dream location and how that might influence your goals for the future.

6. **If you could do absolutely anything with your life, what would you do?** Don't let anything limit your dreaming. If you had all the freedom, time, money, and support you needed, what would you love to do? Open up your imagination and see what comes out.

Answering these questions might help you set goals for the immediate future or long-term aspirations. Whatever the case, working toward them can help you feel good about yourself and less anxious about the future. You might even discover some strong themes that hint at what you want the movie of your life to be about.

I happen to have a lot of rhythm—something I was born with, I guess. I see a gig in a hip-hop act in my future . . . maybe even a recording contract. —Tamir, 14

I have a way with words, writing poetry and stories mostly. For me, writing is like breathing—I need to do it to go on living.
—Liat, 13

I look up to doctors, nurses, first responders, police—basically anyone who goes out of their way to help others. It's important to me that I make that kind of difference.
—Samantha, 15

Life on Earth is not for me—not because I don't like it here but because I'm into space travel. In 10 years I want to be living on the International Space Station.—Bjorn, 14

I'm really worried about the global climate. In my environmental studies course I'm learning a lot about climate change. I think that someday I'll do something to make a big difference for the planet.
—Ricardo, 16

Reaching Your Goals

Setting goals is important, but it's only a first step. You still need a plan to get to where you want to go. You can do this by setting up a series of short-term goals that support the accomplishments you have in mind. When you do this, you're breaking down big challenges into smaller, manageable chunks. Feature films may be impressive when they're all finished and up on the big screen, but they have to be shot one scene at a time.

Five-Step Goal Setting Plan

1. **Write a goal statement.** First and foremost, defining your goal is important. It's hard to accomplish something if you aren't clear about what it is you're trying to do. Be as specific as possible in describing what you want.

2. **Make a list of steps that lead to your goal.** Think about your overall objective and the things you need to do to reach it. These should be small steps that you can comfortably work on without causing stress. (If short-term goals seem impossible or intimidating, you may get frustrated and give up on them.) Keep breaking down goals until they are small enough to be easily accomplished.

3. **List some of the roadblocks you might encounter—and ideas for getting around them.** A lot of people give up on goals when they experience a snag in their plans and just go back to living in the moment. A good way to keep your forward momentum is by anticipating possible problems and coming up with solutions to them before they occur.

4. **List some of the resources that might be helpful toward achieving your goal.** Who can offer insight that will be helpful as you move forward? Are there books or websites that might be good resources? How about local or national organizations with special expertise on a topic? Think of all the different places where you might get information and support.

5. **List the ways you will measure progress toward your goal.**
   It's important to track the progress you're making as you go. If you don't pay attention to this step, it's possible to get off track and do a lot of work that doesn't help—and can even hurt—your efforts. And seeing your progress also can be motivating and give you confidence as you move forward.

> **THE POWER OF GOAL SETTING**
> Writing out your goals may seem like a lot of work, but it's also extremely powerful. Research shows that people who define goals are much more successful at working toward them. The mind is a powerful force, and when you direct it toward the things you want, you have a decisive advantage.

Now that you know about goal setting, let's put it into action to see how it might work in the real world. You can use this same process to outline a plan for reaching something you'd like to accomplish.

REACHING YOUR GOALS

 WRITE A GOAL STATEMENT.

I'd like to get into a college or university program where I can study video game design. During my last year of high school, I will improve my qualifications by getting real-world computer experience.

 MAKE A LIST OF STEPS THAT LEAD TO YOUR GOAL.

I will:

- Do research to learn exactly what a video game designer does.

- Secure an internship with a local tech company.

- Take art classes to improve my drawing skills.

- Find and practice with basic game design software.

- Join a computer club and work on game-related projects with others.
- Do research to learn where online video game design training is offered.

#3 WRITE DOWN SOME OF THE POTENTIAL ROADBLOCKS YOU MIGHT ENCOUNTER—AND IDEAS FOR GETTING AROUND THEM.

What might happen:
- There aren't any internship opportunities near me.
  What I can do: Get involved in a technology mentorship program or see if I can job shadow Joe's mom in her work as a web designer.
- My school doesn't have a computer club.
  What I can do: Start a computer club and find others with my interests.

#4 LIST SOME OF THE RESOURCES THAT MIGHT BE HELPFUL TOWARD ACHIEVING YOUR GOAL.

- Mr. Schmidt in the computer lab.
- Manny, the kid who loves being called a computer geek.
- Ms. Hannover, the guidance counselor.
- Video tutorials about computer game design.
- People in the technology programs at the local community college.

#5 WRITE HOW YOU WILL MEASURE PROGRESS TOWARD YOUR GOAL.

- I'm getting training and experience from an internship or mentor programs.
- I'll work with basic game design software.
- I will learn about game designer jobs and the gaming industry.
- I will have spoken with a counselor at the community college about technical courses and scholarships.
- I have talked to Joe's mom about being a computer programmer and her work life.

Going through this process with each of your goals takes time. But unless you make specific plans, the movie of your life may never be anything more than a daydream—one you at some point wake from and realize you're not where you want to be.

As you work toward goals, remember that the movie of your life is a work in progress. You should feel free to tweak the script and work on goals as your feelings or priorities change. You may want to keep your vision statement and goals in a computer document so you can make changes over time. It's also good to keep in mind that goal setting isn't just for your big life dreams. Use the same five-step goal setting process for the everyday stuff—big and small—to help you get the important things done and reduce stress in your life.

When you know and like where you're going, you'll feel less anxious and more at peace with yourself. You will also feel more in charge of your life and experience the joy, satisfaction, and self-confidence that come from turning your dreams into reality. You'll be working at making your life a mega successful feature film—one in which you are proud to have the starring role.

FIND OUT MORE

Smart Goal Setting for Students (7mindsets.com/smart-goal-setting -for-students). This site offers great tips on how to create and prioritize goals.

Setting and Achieving Goals (goodcharacter.com/BCBC/Goals.html). This site offers step-by-step instructions on how to set appropriate goals and asks questions to guide your goal setting.

Topics to search online:
- Are there TED Talks on goal setting?
- What are some goal setting success stories?
- Where can I learn to be a computer game programmer? (or whatever goal you choose)
- Where can teens find a guide to setting and achieving their goals?

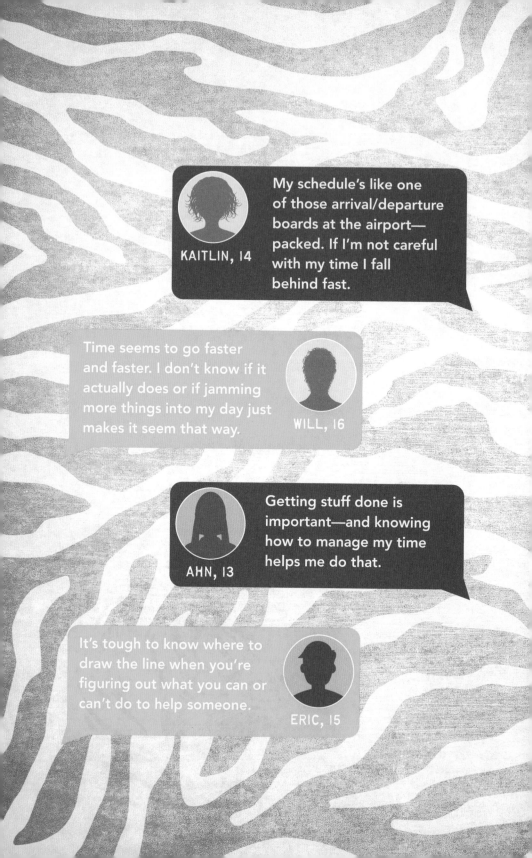

#7

GET TIME ON YOUR SIDE

Say it's Sunday morning and you open your eyes to a blue sky. You imagine an easy day shooting hoops in the park with your friends. Then you remember all the things you have to do: You've got chores around the house, like walking the dog. It's also your mom's birthday next week and you haven't picked up a card. You have your homework—a huge history test on Monday and an English paper due Friday. You also should be preparing for the internship interview you have Wednesday. Oh, and you'd like to replace your favorite ear buds, which the dog mistook for a chew toy. Other than that, you don't have much going on!

Does it seem possible to get all this done and get to the park? Does life feel like an ongoing collection of things to do and you're never caught up? Does it seem like there's not enough time to do all the stuff you have to do, let alone free time for doing other things you enjoy? If you're feeling the pressure of a lot of to-dos, here's a stress-fighting skill that can help: time management.

How Time Management Can Help You

A busy schedule can make it very difficult to get everything done. You can become your own worst invisible tiger by overscheduling and putting too much pressure on yourself. To keep this from happening, use time management skills. These tools can help you stay on top of tasks and make decisions about your schedule, no matter how busy you might be.

GET YOUR SLEEP

If you think skipping sleep is the solution to your time shortage, think again. Experts recommend nine to ten hours of sleep each night for teens—any fewer and you can experience less energy, more stress, poor concentration, and even feelings of sadness or depression. A big part of sleep deprivation is having too much to do—after a full day of school, sports, drama, a job, or other activities, you might not be able to think about homework until it's already late. Another factor: Researchers are finding out what a lot of teens already know—it's often hard for teens to fall asleep until late at night. A teen's biological clock shifts sleep cycles to later hours and makes going to bed early a huge challenge. Lack of a full night of rest can have you sleepwalking through life with invisible stress tigers stalking your every step.

Setting Priorities

One thing time management tools help you do is decide what's important to get done now and what you can do later. Prioritizing tasks and being clear about which things are most important can help you feel more in control of your life and get rid of the stressful feeling that everything needs to be done right now. Try the ABC method, a simple system of prioritization, to bring some order to the chaos of too much to do.

The ABC Method

1. **Start by making a to-do list of all the things you need to get done in the near future.** Include items with firm deadlines (like assignments) as well as regularly occurring events that happen throughout the week—things like spending time with family and friends, shopping, exercise, chores, and anything else you have going on.

ABC TO-DOS: STEP I

Do my chores at home (gardening)
Pick up Mom's birthday card
Study for Monday's history test
Organize track practice with Matt
Work on English paper for Friday
Replace my ear buds
Practice meditating
Call Grandma
Go to a movie with Ann
Prepare for Wednesday's job interview
Email Ms. Robertson
Go for a jog

2. **Now rank each item on your list according to this scale:**
   A—Very important and needs to be done as soon as possible.
   B—Pretty important but can wait until A's are finished.
   C—Nice to do, but not essential.

Let's say, for example, Sunday is the only day to work in the garden with your dad. This makes it a high-priority item—an "A." Working on your English paper is important, but it's not due right away—you could make it a "B." You really like Ann and going to the movie with her would be fun, but it's probably a "C," because it isn't essential to go right away. When you get done, your list might look something like this:

ABC TO-DOS: STEP 2

A. Do my chores at home (gardening)
B. Pick up Mom's birthday card
A. Study for Monday's history test
C. Organize track practice with Matt
B. Work on English paper for Friday
C. Replace favorite ear buds
B. Practice meditating
B. Call Grandma
C. Go to a movie with Ann
A. Prepare for Wednesday's job interview
A. Email Ms. Robertson
C. Go for a jog

3. **Now group all the A's, B's, and C's together.** Once you have them grouped, rank the items in each group individually (since you have several of each). The most important A should be given an A-1 ranking, the next most important A-2, and so on through your list. The last step is to put each group in numerical order. The result would look something like this:

ABC TO-DOS: STEP 3

A-1. Do my chores at home (gardening)
A-2. Study for Monday's history test
A-3. Email Ms. Robertson
A-4. Prepare for Wednesday's job interview
B-1. Pick up Mom's birthday card
B-2. Work on English paper for Friday
B-3. Call Grandma
B-4. Practice meditating
C-1. Organize track practice with Matt
C-2. Go for a jog
C-3. Go to a movie with Ann
C-4. Replace my ear buds

With your to-dos in order, you are much clearer about which items are top priorities and which can wait. When you finish with the A's, you move on to the B's, and then, if you have time, move on to the C's. If you don't have time to do it all after you prioritize your to-dos, you'll at least know that the important things aren't falling through the cracks. You'll also be able to see which activities you can worry less about or eliminate altogether.

Your prioritized list isn't carved in stone, so your challenges may change from one day to the next or, sometimes, from one hour to the next. For example, the due date on your English paper might get pushed back a week, or your friend Ann doesn't have time to see a movie until next weekend. When changes happen, adjust your list of priorities accordingly. What task you tackle next also will depend on what time it is. For example, if it's later in the evening, getting a card for your mom's birthday might not be possible. It might be just the right time, however, to do your meditation exercise.

Your goal is not to accomplish everything on your list. If that's how things work out, great, but don't push yourself too hard. Just do the best you can in the time you've got. At least you'll be getting the important things done and knowing that can relieve a lot of stress.

If you don't prioritize your time, you can be left with a large collection of to-dos and a "do-everything-now-or-else" mentality. Everything seems to demand your attention, which almost guarantees every day will be full of stress and panic. The rest of this section includes more time management strategies to help make you an expert tiger tamer.

Time Management Tips

Give yourself the freedom to say no. People can quickly become overwhelmed when they try to please others and can't say no—whether it's chatting online, helping someone with a project, or just hanging out. It's important to know your limits and turn down invitations when you don't have time. If you feel overbooked and barely have time for the A's on your prioritization list, it's time to start saying "no" to requests for your time. (See pages 56–63 to read more about assertiveness skills.) Also look at the activities toward the bottom of your list for opportunities to free up your schedule. Learning to say "no" shows self-respect and helps you focus on what's important to you.

Know when you're at your best. You can make the best use of time by knowing when you do things well. Some people study best in the early mornings and like to be active in the afternoons. Others like a quiet house later at night for homework and getting as much sleep as possible in the morning. If you know when you're at your best for a given task, try to structure that time in your life . . . and then resist phone calls, texts, emails, and other distractions. When you are following a similar plan each day, you can be more efficient at getting tasks done.

Get your rest. Sleeping might not seem like a way to get things done, but solid rest can help you feel refreshed and ready to take on the day's challenges. When you get enough sleep, your mind is more alert and can perform at its highest level. Your body also will have rested, which keeps you from feeling tired or sluggish.

Schedule breaks. Time management is not about doing something every possible second. Breaks are an important part of staying alert and productive. If you've been hard at work on a paper for a long time, take time to get up, stretch your muscles, and maybe get a snack. A little exercise, like a short walk, is a good way to regain focus. Listening to music or playing with the dog are great for short breaks as long as they don't become giant distractions.

 Beware of time wasters. It's okay to spend some time playing video games, going online, connecting with a friend, or watching TV, but be careful about going overboard. These activities can suck you in for hours at a time. You might innocently flip on the TV or start playing a computer game during a break and not realize how much time is passing—the next thing you know, it's midnight, you're tired, and you don't have your work done.

Use a calendar or planner. You may use an assignment notebook or another scheduling tool at school, but do you have something for tracking other events—like extracurricular activities, social commitments, or family events? A planner lets you see your schedule and know what's ahead so you don't overcommit. You can create a planner using an ordinary notebook, or most mobile phones and email programs have scheduling tools you can use to stay on top of tasks.

When you prioritize and manage your time, you can create order out of stress-filled chaos. Taking charge of your life can give you a sense of accomplishment and build self-esteem. It also helps you stay on top of invisible tigers and make time for something else that's very important—rest and relaxation.

FIND OUT MORE

"Time Management for Teens" (additudemag.com/time-management -for-teens). This article offers tips on effective time management for teens with ADHD.

"13 Time Management Techniques for Teens" (student-tutor.com/blog /time-management-techniques-for-teens). Great information here on getting organized, prioritizing, and keeping everything in line without getting overwhelmed.

Topics to search online:
- How can I say no to requests for my time?
- How much sleep does a teenager need?
- What are good time management apps for teens?

#8

RISK TRYING NEW THINGS

What do you think of when you hear "take a risk"? If you're like many people, you might think of risk-taking as bad, something that can only lead to trouble. While some risks definitely are bad (like using drugs or doing dangerous stunts), positive risk-taking is an important skill that can improve your life and reduce stress. How? Taking risks enables you to explore your interests, learn new things, build your self-esteem, and face difficult challenges. Rather than easing along comfortably, you can push your limits to see what you're capable of.

Are You a Positive Risk-Taker?

Here are a few questions to help you decide if you're a positive risk-taker. Which of the following would you rather do?

- Hang out with your usual friends or introduce yourself to new people?

- Take a course you know is easy or a more interesting one that will be challenging?

- Stick with the same activities after school or try something new?

If you're like many people, the first options probably seem more attractive because they're easy and comfortable. Trying something different can be intimidating. That's because you're taking a risk—a risk that new people won't like you, that you won't do well in a class, that you won't do something well on your first try.

Putting yourself on the line takes courage. You may not know exactly what you're in for, and your current level of knowledge and experience might not be enough to get you through. It's natural to feel uncertain and have a lot of Whatifs ("What if I make a fool of myself onstage?") and Wouldbuts ("I would try out for the team, but I've never played organized sports before"). But choosing not to do something won't enable you to change or grow into your full potential.

THE AMAZING BRAIN

Did you know the human brain is flexible? The brain is made up of billions of neurons that change and adapt when faced with new questions or challenges. Researchers know this from brain scans, which show areas of focused neuron activity in the prefrontal cortex when people are engaged in learning. What does this mean? With study of a subject or practice of a skill, new neural pathways are formed that enable us to be more knowledgeable and efficient at tasks. For example, learning a new language: As the brain is exercised through study and practice, it becomes better at recalling vocabulary. When we push ourselves, we learn and grow.

Start Small and Give Yourself a Chance to Learn

When taking a risk, you don't have to focus on the final outcome right away. Instead, go for the next small step you might take. For example, if you decide that you want to run a marathon, you might not succeed if the race were tomorrow. Marathons are 26.2 miles, that's a long distance even for experienced runners. It doesn't make much sense to enter that race without a lot of preparation. But you can start small—maybe by talking with a coach at school about what goes into running a marathon and setting up a training program to gradually build your endurance. As you prepare and understand more about a challenge, you'll be more ready to take the next step . . . and then the next . . . and the next until you're crossing the finish line.

The point: Small steps are important toward taking risks or trying new things. Continually reaching small milestones keeps you motivated, and the progress you make can give you confidence for meeting future challenges.

Avoiding Perfectionism

Risk-taking can be tough for people who believe they have to succeed right away and be good at everything they do. This is called perfectionism, and it's hard on people because their self-esteem is on the line every minute—which is stressful. Often these people push themselves in all areas of life.

Because it's humanly impossible to be perfect, perfectionism is a guaranteed prescription for feeling like you're not good enough. Many people with perfectionism start to experience depression or hopelessness because they can't live up to their own extreme expectations.

Because perfectionism keeps people from taking risks or trying new things, it is a huge barrier to growing and changing. It also can cause people to slow down. For example, a perfectionist might do the same assignment over and over to make it just right—even though it was done well the first time. While we can all be a little perfectionistic at times, for some people, it affects every part of their lives. To find out how much perfection-ism affects you, take the following quiz. Read each statement and decide how much or how little you agree with it using the number system. You can write numbers on a separate sheet of paper—you'll add them up at the end.

ARE YOU A PERFECTIONIST?

Rating Scale
+2 = Strongly agree
+1 = Somewhat agree
0 = No feeling
-1 = Slightly disagree
-2 = Strongly disagree

1. If I don't set the highest standards for myself, I'll be a failure.
2. People will think less of me if I make mistakes.
3. If I can't do something really well, there's no point in doing it.
4. I get upset if I make a mistake.
5. If I try hard enough, I should be able to excel at anything.
6. It's immature to display any weakness.
7. I shouldn't have to repeat the same mistake more than once.
8. Being average at something isn't satisfying or worthwhile.
9. Failing makes me less of a person.
10. Getting upset about mistakes will help me do better next time.

Five Ways to Fight Perfectionism

When you're done answering the questions, total your score. A score above zero suggests some perfectionistic tendencies. If you have a very high score (like 15–20), life is probably pretty stressful for you. It's important to talk with a parent, counselor, or another trusted adult if you feel this kind of pressure. Here are five ways to fight perfectionism.

1. **Give yourself permission to make mistakes.** Remind yourself that you don't have to be absolutely perfect, we're all human, and it's okay to make mistakes. When you're working on something, think, "I know I may not do this perfectly but that's

okay. Mistakes can help me learn, and doing my best is good enough." Keep repeating this thought as you work.

2. **Set limits on your time.** Do you ever spend too much time trying to do something perfectly? Maybe you have the feeling that no matter how much effort you put into a project, you have to continue working to improve it. To help stop this, think about how long something should take before you start it. Work on the project until you've spent that amount of time, and then stop. If you feel you need to spend more time on something, you can check in with a teacher for an objective opinion on your progress.

3. **Talk yourself out of perfectionistic thinking.** Reduce your negative thoughts by using positive self-talk. One way to do this is to outnumber bad thoughts with good ones. For every negative thought that enters your mind, think of five positive ones. You can learn more about positive self-talk on page 111.

4. **Address perfectionism in your family.** Often teens "inherit" their perfectionistic traits from parents or other family members. Maybe adults around you are perfec- tionists, and you've learned the behavior. Or perhaps you feel like the people around you expect your performance in school or other activities to be perfect. If you're living with a feeling of "never good enough," it's important to talk with an adult you trust— someone not pressuring you—to get perspective on the situation and ideas for bringing up the subject with those you live with.

5. **Give yourself a break.** It's natural to want to do your best at school and in other activities. But it's also important to do some things that are just for fun. Put yourself in situations where you're not worried about how well you're doing, but instead are simply enjoying an activity. Take a walk, watch a movie, throw a Frisbee, call a family member, or anything else that you enjoy doing.

GOOD OR BAD RISK?
How can you tell if a risk is good or bad? Think of the worst possible outcome. Will your or anyone else's safety be in danger? Will property be destroyed? Is it illegal? Will anyone's feelings be hurt? If the answer is yes to any of these questions, it's a bad risk. If the worst thing that could happen is a little embarrassment, the risk is probably a positive one you can take. For more on measuring risks, see "Stand on Solid Ground" (pages 101–107).

20 POSITIVE WAYS TO CHALLENGE YOURSELF

1. form a club
2. make new friends
3. run for student government
4. ask for help to build a work résumé
5. speak up in class
6. take challenging courses
7. stand up for yourself
8. join the school play
9. walk away from a fight
10. start a blog
11. enter a talent contest
12. try out for a team
13. form a music group
14. say no, even if it's hard to do
15. volunteer with a neighborhood organization
16. make your own comic book
17. share your creative writing with others
18. become a mentor
19. join the school band
20. try baking something

Find Support and Celebrate Successes

Taking risks doesn't mean going it alone with no help from others. In fact, it's important to get encouragement and advice from people. Parents, stepparents, grandparents, aunts, uncles, friends, neighbors, members of the community, professionals working in a certain field, and others you trust can support you if you encounter any obstacles. There may still be times when things don't work out the way you plan, but these people can help you get back on track. Risk-taking and support go hand in hand.

It's also important to celebrate your successes, even if they seem small. Big achievements don't usually happen overnight. Instead, they are the result of smaller accomplishments over a longer period of time. Steps you complete in areas that are new to you deserve to be acknowledged and celebrated—they're proof of your progress toward your goals and they're great motivators. You might even design a reward system for your accomplishments by doing nice things for yourself at steps along the way.

FIND OUT MORE

Mentor: The National Mentoring Partnership (mentoring.org). Looking for people to support you in life? Log on to this website to learn about mentoring agencies in your community.

Topics to search online:
- What does it mean to leave my comfort zone?
- What are some positive risks to take in high school?
- What are the dangers of perfectionism for a teen?
- Why do perfectionists procrastinate?

STAND ON
SOLID GROUND

Can you imagine what it would be like to experience an earth-
quake with everything around you in motion—buildings teetering
back and forth, the pavement under your feet shifting up, down,
sideways? Now imagine living that way for a long time, the earth
constantly moving under your feet, always feeling anxious and
unsure of what you should do next. Not knowing what decisions to
make during stressful times can feel a lot like standing on shaky
ground. Decision-making skills can help you find some solid personal ground and reduce the amount of stress you feel.

Decisions Are Powerful

Most of life comes down to the decisions you make. What you decide to do helps determine whether good or bad things will happen. When you were younger, your family and other people made a lot of decisions for you. While you probably still get guidance from adults and have rules to follow, getting older means making more of your own choices. But with these new freedoms also comes more responsibility. It's not always easy to know what decision to make—especially when you might be feeling pressure from someone. That's why it's important to remember the bottom line on decisions—every single one matters.

GOOD OR BAD DECISION?

1. Will anyone be put in danger?
2. Will anyone be disrespected or insulted?
3. Will anyone's property be stolen or damaged?
4. Will this decision make a situation worse?
5. Will I be breaking any laws?
6. Will I have to lie about something?
7. Will I be escalating a conflict?
8. Will I get in trouble with my family, my school, or the law?
9. Will I be letting people down?
10. Will I feel bad about myself afterward?

Unless you can absolutely, positively answer no to each
question, you should seriously consider whether your decision
is a good one. It's also a good idea to get the advice of a parent,
counselor, trusted friend, mentor, or another adult when making a
big decision.

Making Decisions When the Pressure's On

A lot of things can get in the way of making a good decision—
including strong feelings. Anger and other powerful emotions can
cause us to react in destructive ways when we're in a tough situation. Often, when we lose control and act without thinking, we can
resort to using violence, swearing, yelling, making threats, using
put-downs, breaking things, or defying authority figures.

What can you do to keep a clear head when someone's pushing you or you feel like you might lose control?

10 Tips for Tough Situations

1. **Step out.** Just for a moment, step out of the situation, take a few
   deep breaths, and try to collect your thoughts. Count down
   from 10, promising yourself you won't do or say anything until
   you reach zero.

2. **Consider options.** List three options for yourself . . . three
   different ways in which you could address the situation. Having
   a few choices increases the likelihood you'll make the best
   decision in the moment. If you have time, it's always good to
   talk with others you trust to get perspective and help coming
   up with solutions to problems.

3. **Visualize consequences.** Think about the possible consequences of your decision—what's the absolute worst thing that
   could result from responding in the wrong way? Will someone
   be hurt? Will you get in trouble? Imagine yourself in the
   situation—what will it feel like for you or how will people react?

4. **Retaliation makes things worse.** If your behavior is a reaction out of anger to what someone said or did, it's likely you won't make a good decision. Just because someone did something foolish does not give you a free pass to get revenge. Instead, recognize when someone's pushing you. Stay strong, be smart, and don't lose your cool.

5. **Ignore put-downs.** If someone's putting you down, either to your face or behind your back, don't pay attention. Let people ruin their own reputations if they want to but refuse to lower yourself to their level. Often others will lose interest when they see you're unaffected by their behavior.

6. **Use positive self-talk.** How we talk to ourselves can influence our actions and feelings when we're facing a tough choice. If you're feeling the stress of a difficult decision, you can say to yourself, "I'm feeling upset right now, but I can stay calm and handle this situation in a positive way." Thinking you're in control can help you stay in control.

7. **Use I-messages.** If you're experiencing conflict with someone, instead of casting blame and potentially escalating conflicts, use I-messages as you work to resolve problems. I-messages work really well for presenting your case to authority figures. Instead of storming out of a classroom you might say something like, "I feel upset that I'm being blamed for what happened and would like to talk about it."

8. **Talk to someone.** Some situations benefit from another perspective. Talking through your decision with a good listener can help clarify things for you. Speak with a family adult, teacher, or other trusted adult about anything that's giving you a hard time.

9. **Walk away.** Sometimes leaving is the best solution to a difficult situation. Split, boogie, depart, get out, hit the road. A little time and distance can provide the perspective you need. Most big challenges, of course, eventually will have to be addressed, but finding some time, space, and room to breathe in stressed moments can help you rethink a situation.

10. **Recognize when you're losing control.** Most of us have some sense of when we're feeling highly upset and on the verge of doing something we'll regret. Try to recognize these feelings in yourself and take a break when you need one. When you're on your own, you might use focused breathing (page 42), positive self-talk, or another technique from this book to cool down.

Managing Peer Pressure

Does it sometimes seem like everyone thinks they know what's best for you? If it's not adults, it's friends—"You'll have fun at this party" or "You'll totally like this guy." And you might. But you also might not, and you might be put in a position where you feel pressure to do something you're not interested in or comfortable doing.

It's natural to want to be liked; nobody wants to be uncool, looked down on, or excluded. That's why peer pressure can be so persuasive. Here are some suggestions for standing your ground when the pressure's on.

Play it straight. Be pleasant, straightforward, and tell people what you don't want to do. Ask them to stop pressuring you. You can give a reason for your decision, but you don't have to explain yourself.

"I don't want to smoke. End of discussion."

"You can all go ahead. My mom's expecting me home."

Offer another suggestion. Offering an alternative can get you off the hot seat without risking a confrontation. As long as you're comfortable with the new idea, everyone can win.

"I'm not really down for a fight with those guys tonight. Let's get something to eat instead."

"I'm not going to post anything about Sara. Let's put up a list of fashion tips instead."

Make a joke or change the subject. Joking or changing the topic of conversation can get you past some uncomfortable, pressure-packed moments. It's a gentle way to let someone know you're not interested in where the conversation or action is headed.

"No way. That stuff makes people act like zombies."

"Nah, I don't want to do that. But, hey, are you going to the game Thursday night?"

Sometimes even someone you are very close with will try to influence your thoughts and actions. If you're feeling a lot of pressure to behave in ways that make you uncomfortable, it's important to talk about it with that person. Describe the pressure you feel and what changes you'd like to happen. (You might use the ASSERT Formula on pages 57–63 for this discussion.) Your good friends will listen and accept your decisions.

THE IMPULSIVE BRAIN

Researchers have learned that the brain continues to develop for a longer period of time than previously thought—it's not until one reaches their mid-20s that the brain is fully formed. One part that is undergoing rapid development during the teen years is the prefrontal cortex—the region of the brain responsible for reasoning and impulse control. Because the prefrontal cortex is under construction, teens can be attracted to risky situations and make quick decisions without thinking about the consequences of their actions.

FIND OUT MORE

Above the Influence (abovetheinfluence.com). Stories from real teens, games, and advice make this site a one-stop source of information for dealing with peer pressure.

"Teens and Peer Pressure" (teens.webmd.com/peer-pressure#1). This article at WebMD offers terrific, straightforward advice on how to react when facing unwanted pressure.

Topics to search online:
- At what age is the human brain fully developed?
- What does the prefrontal cortex do?
- What is executive function in a teen's brain?
- How do hormones affect behavior?
- What is body scanning?

CHOOSE THE UPSIDE VIEW

Stress can make you feel anxious and eat away at your self-esteem. When you're at the limit of your ability to cope, it can seem like you're lost in the stress jungle and your life will never get better. But a few other skills can be helpful when it feels like invisible tigers are gaining on you. These techniques take almost no effort, are totally free, and have an instant payback. They're about making a choice to see the upside view of life.

Seeing the Upside

"Seeing the upside" means remembering all the good things about you and your life. While this may sound too simple to be effective, it truly works. After all, stress is a reaction to how you perceive the world, so how you view and think about the world affects how you feel. Have you ever been down or depressed about something, maybe even something small, and it grew and grew in your thoughts until it seemed like a huge problem? Focusing attention on anxious or frightening thoughts is like looking at them with a magnifying glass. When you do that, they appear much bigger than they really are, and then it's easy and natural to feel overwhelmed and out of control. Focusing on the negative is a sure way to become your own worst invisible stress tiger.

The opposite is true too. When you have a positive attitude about yourself and your life, the world is a less stressful place. Instead of dwelling on the negative things that might happen, you can focus on your strengths and abilities to overcome challenges. It's true sad events or stressful situations will still occur and you'll have to deal with them, but when you can see the upside, the good things inside you, and the people who care about you, you're in a much stronger position to deal with tough times. That's why people often say that life is all about having the right attitude.

How do you begin to see the upside?

In the same way you strengthen your muscles by lifting weights, you can have a more positive attitude by practicing upside thoughts. Think about the great parts of your life and write them in a list. Include things you like and the people you care about. You might also list your talents, accomplishments, and anything else you appreciate or are proud of.

THE POWER OF POSITIVITY

Positive thinking has a powerful effect on your body. Research shows that people who are optimistic not only have better mental health, but also better physical health. Optimism can help your heart and lungs stay healthy and strengthen your immune system so that you are sick less often. It's even been shown that people with serious illnesses live longer when they have a sense of humor and a brighter outlook on life.

THINGS I'M THANKFUL FOR

- a comfortable place to sleep at night
- good food—especially pasta with pesto and mushrooms
- my health
- my family
- my science skills
- my cat
- my favorite hoodie
- Tom, Ricardo, and the guys
- my kindness toward others
- our soccer team's domination
- living in a free country

After you're done, take a close look at your list. It's important to recognize all the things that are right with you and your life. Keep your list on hand and review it often. Add to it when new things come up.

Positive Self-Talk

We all talk to ourselves constantly, whether we realize it or not. If we actually had these conversations out loud, it would seem very weird—and we might not like hearing what comes out of our mouths. What we say to ourselves has a big impact on how we feel. Positive self-talk is another way to train yourself to choose the upside view.

SEEING THE POSITIVE

INSTEAD OF: "I'm so overweight. It's no wonder other kids tease me all the time."

TRY: "I'm a good person and deserve to be treated with respect."

INSTEAD OF: "I'll never be able to improve my grades."

TRY: "I'm smart and willing to work hard. I can work with my teachers to do better at school."

INSTEAD OF: "Other kids don't like me because I spaz out sometimes."

TRY: "I have many good qualities and have a lot to share with others."

INSTEAD OF: "I can't do anything right and deserve to be miserable."

TRY: "I'm a unique person with a lot of talents. I want and deserve a great life."

INSTEAD OF: "Things are out of control—I won't be able to get my life back on track."

TRY: "I can handle my problems by making good decisions and getting help from others."

INSTEAD OF: "I'd like to learn tae kwon do, but I don't think I'll be any good at it."

TRY: "I have a lot of determination and with a good instructor I can succeed."

Replacing negative thoughts with positive ones can make a big difference in how you feel about yourself and your life. The key is to do it consistently—whenever you hear a negative thought in your head, replace it with a positive one. When you do, you can be your own best friend, build confidence, and tame invisible tigers.

Lighten Up

Another approach to seeing the upside is to see the humorous side of life. It's understandable that we're sometimes stressed or fearful about what's happening in our lives. And it's natural to be worried about troubling local and world events. But always feeling anxious or afraid is unhealthy. That's why it's important to lighten up whenever we can—to smile and laugh and put things in perspective.

Scientists have known for a long time that humor has positive physical and emotional benefits. Laughter increases respiratory activity (breathing rate), oxygen exchange, muscular activity, and heart rate. It also stimulates the pituitary gland, which leads to an overall positive biochemical state. Simply put, humor is good for you. You might try smiling right now and see what happens!

Sometimes it can be hard to laugh, like during very stressful periods or when something bad has happened. People who are very shy may also have a hard time showing a lighter side. You have the right to respond in your own way in these situations but remember the old saying: Laughter is the best medicine. Here are some suggestions to lighten up.

Five Ways to Lighten Up

1. **Hang out with people who are happy and who have a good sense of humor.** Being around someone who's positive and funny can give you a lift. Make sure your personal safety net includes these people. (See pages 65–73 for more about your personal safety net.)

2. **Watch movies and TV shows you know will make you feel happy.** If you have a choice between a comedy or feel-good film and a movie that's very sad or disturbing, choose the one more likely to improve your spirits.

3. **Search the internet for hilarious film clips and funny sites.** Spread the cheer by sharing what you find with family members and friends.

4. **Many people have a favorite comic strip or cartoon they like to read each day.** A variety of these can be found online.

5. **Learn one joke a week and share it with people you know.** Even if some of the jokes are corny and cause groans from people, this habit can be a fun way to get others laughing—and to get them to share jokes of their own.

Seeing the upside view is important for feeling good about yourself. It helps you stay positive and keep things in perspective when life is particularly stressful or challenging. If you're skeptical, try using one of these methods for a day to see what happens. Learning to live on the upside can help you feel better in a hurry.

FIND OUT MORE

GoComics (gocomics.com). Visit this site to read many syndicated comic strips including *Calvin and Hobbes, F Minus,* and many more. You can even have cartoons emailed to you every day.

Topics to search online:
- What is gratitude?
- What chemicals are released in the brain when I laugh?
- What are the effects of optimism on mental health?

#11
MANAGE DIGITAL TIGERS

In addition to our physical lives (doing chores, going to school, and so on), we have a whole other digital life online. We can access all the knowledge of the world immediately. We can play video games with friends who live across town and never leave our own bedrooms. We have instant (and constant) contact with friends, family, and acquaintances nearly anywhere on the planet. Yet while the digital world is full of ways to create a great life, the same technology comes with real-world stress that impacts the kids (and adults) who use it. Soon, we can find ourselves surrounded by . . . digital tigers!

Digital tigers are very sneaky. You might think checking social media or texting with friends in a group chat helps you relax and forget the tigers you already face. But research shows that today's teens—who've never known a life without screens around them 24-7—are experiencing higher levels of anxiety, depression, and loneliness than other generations who didn't have constant access to the internet their whole lives. In other words: We created a digital world with just as many stressors as the real one!

Like anything, being online has its plusses and minuses. It's only recently that science has begun to understand some of the negatives of having a large digital component to your life. You've heard about drug addiction. This can happen when you regularly take a drug and your body starts to crave it. This often leads to other side effects that can damage the body if you continue to take the drug. The same thing can happen in the digital world.

In a 2016 survey by Common Sense Media, half of the teens who responded said they feel like they're addicted to their digital devices. They felt like they *needed* to "immediately respond to texts, social media posts, and other notifications." Another study showed that people who play a lot of computer and video games—more than three hours a day—have brain scan patterns similar to those of people addicted to drugs.

While spending some time online can be helpful—you can research a paper for school, catch up with friends, or stream songs from your favorite artist—spending too much time with a screen in your face can pull you into a digital jungle where a whole new pack of tigers lie in wait. And if you're not careful, screen time can start to replace time that could be used for other important activities: being outdoors, staying physically active, and interacting in-person with family and friends.

For more information about online addiction, search for On-Line Gamers Anonymous. They have information to help screen-addicted people manage their screen habits and reconnect with real people and the outside world.

Watching for Digital Tigers

Because we tend to think of the digital world as something we can turn on and off as we choose, we often don't realize how much power and control our screens have over us. And when our defenses are down like that, the digital tigers wait for a chance to pounce.

Here are some questions to ask yourself if you're wondering if you're becoming digitally dependent:

- Do you ever feel like you're spending too much time with screens, or do you hear that from the adults around you?

- Do you get upset, angry, or stressed if your screen time is cut off or limited?

- Does what you are doing online add stress, anxiety, or drama to your life?

- Do you spend time on screens when you could be having real face time with family or friends? Do you prefer connecting online instead of in person?

- Would you feel lost without a smartphone, a tablet, or an internet connection for an hour? How about a whole day? A week?

- Do you lose track of time online and have problems with things like not getting your homework done or ignoring your home responsibilities?

- Is online gaming becoming a habit, or worse, a need? Do you feel like you arrange your day so you can get back to gaming as soon as possible? Is it the first thing you do after school?

- Have you tried to spend less time online but failed and found yourself back in front of your screens? Have you ever lied to anyone about how much time you spend online?

If you said yes to more than three of these questions, you're at risk for screen-driven stress. Spending most of your time in the two-dimensional world of screens can make it more difficult to improve your life, strengthen your friendships, move toward your life's goals, or become a happier person. It might be time to rethink your relationship to screens.

Taming Digital Tigers

If you're at even a little risk for being consumed by your screens, here are some suggestions for understanding the dangers, being intentional about how you manage them, and navigating the digital jungle.

Avoid digital junk food. If your online life consists of general playing around, killing time, constantly checking likes, reading other people's posts, or learning about all the bad news in the world, it's exactly like eating junk food. It's okay sometimes but consuming too much digital anything is a diet that's not good for you in the long run.

Have you heard the term FOMO? It stands for **F**ear **O**f **M**issing **O**ut. This can occur when you spend much of your time following the online lives of other people (mostly strangers). You can start to feel like your life is not as wonderful as all the fun and exciting things others are posting about. This can actually decrease your sense of well-being. Or maybe you feel competitive and stressed about getting as many likes as the posts of others. You could also feel like you're not as popular or connected as other (heavy) social media users.

Screen time can give you a temporary distraction from your real life, create the illusion that you're doing something that counts, and give you some not very nourishing connections to others. But ultimately, too much digital junk food is going to make you unhappy, lonely, and hungry for something substantial. The digital world can be terrific. But just like going to a huge supermarket, you have to know what's good for you and what's not . . . and then make good choices.

Put humans before screens. We are social creatures and while online interaction with people creates the illusion of connection, it's not always a good substitute for personal interaction. You don't have to give up online relationships. But you may want to consider reducing the amount of time you spend conversing on a screen and increasing face-to-face time with people. True friendships come from having extended in-person time together, talking about your life in more depth, and sharing feelings.

Separate fact from fiction. IRL is online shorthand that means "in real life." It's how people talk about their day-to-day interactions in the non-digital world. The fact that we call it "real life" suggests we know there's something *not* real about the time we spend online. But it can sometimes be hard to tell the difference, especially when it comes to relationships.

And remember, not everything online is how it appears. You probably know by now that you can't believe everything on the internet. You've heard of fake news (alleged news sites that create false stories without evidence to back up their claims) and you know that *anyone* can edit a Wikipedia page to say anything they want. The same is true for how people present themselves online.

The next time you find yourself admiring people's lives based on the pictures or information they post, remember they're only showing you the good stuff they want you to see. But everyone has problems. They just don't show them online. In fact, showing off online might be a way that they're trying to deal with their problems. The point is: Don't believe everything that people—especially people you've never met—tell you about themselves in the digital world. No one's life is that perfect.

Avoid toxic people. Some people are just not good for you, in person or online. These are people who embarrass you or create drama and stress by what they say or post about you or others online. Toxic people are people who send you messages that make you feel uncomfortable, are hurtful, or increase fear and stress. They might break into your accounts and create fake posts by you. They might extort, bully, or pressure you with threats that they'll post your private material. Or they might not leave you alone and instead smother you with digital activity. These people are like poison that can make you sick and stressed, and they need to be avoided at all costs.

If people who are toxic contact you online, don't respond. If that doesn't work, the most important thing you can do is cut them off, block their access, and change your privacy settings. If you're still under attack, get adult support to help you deal with them. Like with any kind of poison, taking immediate action when dealing with someone who's toxic will de-stress your online experience and greatly improve your life.

Take a screen vacation. If just the mention of not using your screens for a while makes you uncomfortable, it might mean you *really do* need some time away. Think about it: What have you stopped doing as a result of the amount of time you spend with screens? What parts of your life could you pump up if you put down your screens for an hour each day, or after 7 p.m., or for a whole day, or even for a week? Just like taking a real vacation to some far-off, exotic location, there's a good chance you'd come back rested and happy.

Taking charge of your screens. Instead of allowing screens to control your life, you can be intentional about screen time management. Here are some ways you can change your relationship to screens:

- The first step in managing your screens is to figure out how much time you spend on screens. For a whole day, pay attention to, or even keep track of, how many times you check your smartphone for texts, messages, or social networking updates. Record how much time you spend watching videos or playing online games. When you get a sense for how much you're involved with screens you can then begin to make some choices to get in charge of screen time.

> Search your favorite app store for "digital wellness" or "screen time." You'll find many apps to help you monitor your screen time and even, if you choose, let you lock yourself out for short periods of time.

- Don't use your favorite digital device for a few hours. Go non-digital for a while to see how it feels. In the beginning, you might feel uncomfortable not filling time with a screen. It might feel like withdrawal. To push past that feeling, try being creative with this time. Enjoy a book, go for a run, or practice a mindfulness activity (see chapter 3).

- Create a screen-time budget. Give yourself a limited amount of time online each day. Or set limits on when you can use screens, for example, not before school starts and not after 10 p.m. Start small, see what happens, and then adjust.

Practice safe screen use. Earlier, we discussed that not everything in the digital world is always what it seems. This includes people. You don't know if what they tell you about themselves online is the truth. You can't be sure how old they are or even if their photo is really of them. This is a dangerous part of the digital jungle. Here are a few things you can do to practice safe screen use:

- Don't use the web to measure popularity. Some people have an obsessive need to have the most friends or followers. But having a ton of anonymous followers online is a false way to feel good about yourself. Also, it can be dangerous. It has nothing to do with having real friends and it can lead to feeling lonely and disconnected.

- Learn to use privacy settings to allow only approved online connections to see your information and lock out anyone you don't know.

- Don't give out any personal identifying information or make it easy for people to find you in real life. Limit what you say about yourself in public profiles. Don't ever give out your address, phone number, or even the name of your school. This is especially true for photos. Be careful of the types of pictures you post to the digital world or text to people. **Anything you put online will be there forever.** And never, ever share your password.

- There are people who spend time online solely to take advantage of others, especially kids and teens. They'll offer to listen to your problems and it may seem like they really understand what you're going through. But, remember, even someone who seems nice might not be who they say they are. If they ask you to send nude photos or offer to meet you somewhere so you can talk in person, this person probably doesn't have your best interests in mind. Report online behavior like this to a trusted adult immediately. And steer clear of online pornography. Porn sites are home to online predators and are known for malware, spyware, and viruses that can infect your system.

- If you're riding in a car and the driver is texting, tell the driver you don't feel safe. Explain that texting while driving is dangerous (and may be illegal), and you would like the texting to stop. More than 1.5 million car accidents and almost a half-million injuries a year are the result of texting. You don't want to be one of those statistics.

FIND OUT MORE

Got NetSmartz? (cdn.netsmartz.org/tipsheets/tips_for_teens.pdf). This tip sheet offers solid advice for taking precautions online, especially when dealing with people you don't know in real life.

"Teen Internet Safety Tips" (teens.webmd.com/features/teen-internet -safety-tips#1). These tips from medical professionals show you how to keep yourself safe online.

Topics to search online:
- What are the effects of screen time on brain development?
- What are the stats for teen texting and driving?
- Find a quick self-assessment on internet addiction.

FIRST AID FOR TIGER BITES

It's frightening to feel at the limit of what you can handle. First of all, remember that you're not alone. Many people feel overwhelmed, scared, lost, or depressed during difficult times. The important thing is to recognize when you need help and act in positive ways to help yourself feel better.

When Is It Time to Get Help?

Knowing the signs of stress overload is important so you know when to reach out for help. Here are the signals:

Always feeling angry. If it seems like you're mad a lot of the time, built-up tension could be affecting your mood. You might also get into more arguments with teachers, classmates, and people in your house.

Changes in sleeping habits. If you're under a lot of pressure, you might have trouble getting or staying asleep. Or maybe you want to sleep all the time. Problems with sleep are one way your body tells you something is wrong.

Changes in eating habits. Stress can affect appetite. Some people experiencing anxiety lose their appetite. Others want to eat everything in sight. Eating and feeling full can change your body chemistry and temporarily mask the effects of stress.

Aches, pains, and increased sickness. Ongoing stress weakens the immune system and can cause a variety of health problems. Some health concerns that are often stress-related include headaches, stomachaches, sore muscles, colds, missed menstrual cycles, and infections.

Escapist behaviors. Overdoing things like playing video games, listening to music, exercising, using social media, using substances, studying, and sleeping can mean you're stuck in a vicious circle of stress avoidance (see page 13). Hours and hours of these activities not only causes you to miss out on other fun experiences, but also adds to the stress you feel.

Withdrawing from family members and friends. Always wanting to be alone is a very serious sign that something is wrong. It's when you're feeling your worst that you most need the important people in your life.

Feeling nervous, frightened, or worried all the time. Stress can make you feel constantly on edge—like something bad could happen any moment. Some people even experience panic attacks, which are sudden feelings of overwhelming anxiety that come without warning or any obvious reason. These feelings can wear you down and suck up so much of your energy that even everyday tasks become difficult to handle.

Crying often and for no apparent reason. Crying when you're upset about an event is normal and a positive way to process sad feelings. But if you find yourself feeling sad, hopeless, or crying a lot, it's time to get help.

Using alcohol or other drugs. Drinking alcohol, smoking cigarettes, or using other drugs are definite signals that a person needs help. These substances harm your body, create lots of additional consequences, and ultimately make you feel worse.

Feeling out of control. For many people on stress overload, the world seems to spin faster and faster until they feel they can no longer hang on. It's like you've lost your grip on the things that keep you anchored in what is right about yourself and your life. It's a terrifying feeling that generates its own stress.

Feeling depressed or wanting to harm yourself. Not being able to handle all the challenges in your life can lead to depression, unhealthy risks, and self-harming behaviors. If you feel hopeless about life or like you want to hurt yourself in any way, first, don't do it! Instead, find the courage to reach out and talk to someone you trust right away.

Things to Remember . . .

You are lovable, valuable, and important to many people. This is true even when you are feeling your worst. Desperate thinking and self-destructive behaviors are signals that you are up against more than you can handle at this point in your life. They mean you need help, support, and objectivity from people you trust. Here are some things to keep in mind as you work to heal tiger bites:

It's okay to admit you need help. One of the biggest challenges can be admitting we're in trouble. It's often hard to acknowledge life isn't working out right now or that we've made some bad decisions. But not admitting that we're having difficulties—to ourselves or others—is denial. Denial allows us to fool ourselves into thinking we're handling things better than we really are. To really feel better, it's important to admit we need help. It can take real courage and strength, but it's the only doorway to a better life.

People you trust want to help. When we're struggling with challenges, it can seem like we're troubling others by opening up and sharing with them. This thinking leads to feeling more and more isolated over time. You deserve and can find allies. Don't let this false notion that you're bothering others keep you from reaching out in your time of greatest need. Parents, other family members, friends, spiritual leaders, school counselors, teachers, and other people you trust want to support you. They can provide a safe environment where you have permission to be your mixed-up, confused, lost, or even weird self. People we trust accept us no matter what and can help us find ways to overcome challenges. If one person doesn't seem to take your worries seriously or to be able to help, reach out to another. Don't stop reaching out until someone takes your concerns seriously.

Stop negative coping behaviors. Coping behaviors help us avoid uncomfortable feelings that come with the difficult challenges. But they are only short-term solutions that can make things worse and don't address the root problems causing stress. Negative coping behaviors (like isolating yourself or using alcohol or other drugs) are destructive. Stopping them is important for feeling better. Even if people around you are stuck in destructive behaviors, you can reach out to others you trust who can help.

Plan to deal with big personal issues. At some point, many of us will have to face and deal with the really sad or difficult parts of our lives. Whether it's a problem with drinking or violence at home, abuse, the death of a family member or friend, bullying, a disability, or any other difficult situation, it's important to address what's going on for you. If you feel like you're a victim of what's happening, it's easy to feel terrified, confused, ashamed, sad, or hopeless. Don't wait until that happens. Reach out for the help and support you need as soon as you realize you need it.

IMPORTANT!

You are not alone! If you don't feel like there's anyone you can talk to, there are other caring people you can call who are waiting to listen and support you. These calls are anonymous, confidential, and free.

Here are a few numbers:

Teen Line (1-800-TLC-TEEN). This is a hotline where you can talk with a trained teen who will help you work things out. It's staffed from 6:00 to 10:00 p.m. PST. Or check out their website at teenlineonline.org.

National Suicide Prevention Lifeline (1-800-273-8255). The Lifeline provides 24-7 support for people in distress.

Boys Town National Hotline (1-800-448-3000). This hotline is staffed 24 hours a day, 365 days a year with counselors who want to help.

A FINAL WORD

I hope what you've learned about stress and the many stress management skills you can acquire will help you become more grounded, calm, confident, happy, and stress-resilient. I hope you'll find it easier to get through the hard times and that the "jungle" of your life will become less threatening. I hope you will experience more of the joys and satisfactions that are possible and that you'll always treat yourself with the same kindness and caring you'd want from a best friend.

Finally, I hope you find the courage to dream big dreams and go after what you really want. You deserve the very best. By taking great care of yourself and using the stress management skills in this book to manage the hurdles, I know you can put together an amazing life.

My best wishes go with you.

Earl Hipp

INDEX

About the Author

Earl Hipp is the author of many books for young people. He has a bachelor's degree in psychology and a master's in psychophysiology. Earl was previously a clinical psychotherapist, where he helped people understand, cope with, and grow through some of the big challenges in their lives. An experienced speaker and trainer, he is available to speak to groups on the subjects of his books. Earl also enjoys hearing from his readers and can be reached at help4kids@freespirit.com.